MANAGING
THE NEW
BOTTOM LINE

ISSUES
MANAGEMENT
FOR SENIOR
EXECUTIVES

MANAGING THE NEW BOTTOM LINE

ISSUES MANAGEMENT FOR SENIOR EXECUTIVES

Raymond P. Ewing

DOW JONES-IRWIN
Homewood, Illinois   60466

This publication is designed to provide accurate and
authoritative information in regard to the subject matter
covered. It is sold with the understanding that the
publisher is not engaged in rendering legal, accounting, or
other professional service. If legal advice or other expert
assistance is required, the services of a competent
professional person should be sought.

*From a Declaration of Principles jointly adopted by a Committee
of the American Bar Association and a Committee of Publishers.*

This book was set in Century Schoolbook by The Saybrook Press, Inc.
The editors were Margaret S. Haywood and Merrily D. Mazza.
The production manager was Irene H. Sotiroff.
The designer was Stuart Paterson.
The drawings were done by John Foote.
Arcata Graphics/Kingsport was the printer and binder.

ISBN 0-87094-973-X

Library of Congress Catalog Card No. 87–70726

Printed in the United States of America

1 2 3 4 5 6 7 8 9 0 K 4 3 2 1 0 9 8 7

DEDICATION

This book is dedicated to the last four Chairmen and CEOs of the Allstate Insurance Companies, each of whom contributed in his own way to the evolution of the concept of issues management and the author's understanding of it:

Judson B. Branch—1966–1972
Archie R. Boe—1972–1982
Donald F. Craib, Jr.—1982–1986
Richard J. Haayen—1986–

They grounded public policy management in vision *and* business realities, measured performance in both economic and ethical terms. However, the reader is cautioned to not attribute the author's opinions and judgments expressed in this book to them. They are his alone, in keeping with Allstate's tradition of encouraging independent thinking.

Every successful corporate executive is judged in the end by the bottom line his or her enterprise posts year after year. For most of this century, the bottom line was defined exclusively in terms of profit earned for the benefit of the stockholders.

However, business leaders began to realize that this bottom line was determined and conditioned by factors outside of the market place. In fact, during the last two decades, we have come to realize that we have a broader bottom line—one the author of this book calls the "new bottom line." He is right.

Profitability is still absolutely central to the modern corporation's bottom line, but so is high-quality performance that meets the needs of customers, employees, and the public. Profit and public acceptance are so interrelated that neither is achievable without the other.

A case in point is the reborn Chrysler Corporation. When new leadership took over, Chrysler faced bankruptcy, customer disinterest, low employee morale, stockholder abandonment, fierce foreign competition, and public contempt. Its new CEO and senior management team knew Chrysler's bottom line wasn't merely achieving profit goals, but achieving public acceptance— new employee morale, customers' faith and satisfaction, investor support, and public approval—while it set out to meet the competition and achieve its profit goals. The record shows that Chrysler's executives not only met the rigorous standards of the new bottom line for modern corporations, but did so with such forward-looking success that they are now able to expand production capacity and product line by acquiring another foundering auto maker. The old Chrysler faced failure and bankruptcy by concentrating exclusively on the old bottom line—profits. It failed. The new Chrysler recognized the new bottom line and devoted the energy of its management to achieving broader realities. It succeeded.

Of course, many outstanding executives of the past intuitively knew the importance of public acceptance to the success of their companies. However, only since the 1970s have corporate leaders developed new planning techniques to guide their companies consciously and firmly toward the goals of the new bottom line. These management tools are strategic planning and issues management—profit planning and public policy planning for the corporation. The two planning methods use similar tools, interact, and are totally focused on the bottom line—the real bottom line of the corporation.

This book concentrates on the issues management process and its value to the modern corporation. It fills a gap in the literature of planning because many corporate executives have an incomplete understanding of what issues management is and how valuable it can be to them and their companies. Many still confuse strategic business planning with issues management. The author carefully explains their differences and similarities. He also discusses the different types of staff professionals required to develop work products for senior executives to consider and make informed judgments in arriving at key planning decisions for their companies. Having discussed and debated these distinctions with him over an eight-year period, I am sure you will find his reasoning persuasive. In any event, I did in most cases—although I do foresee a time when staff managers will be proficient in both strategic business planning and issues management.

I would like to call the reader's attention to Chapter 3, the Evolution of the Modern Corporation. It is an interesting effort to describe the modern corporation in its broadest dimensions. In a sense, it is a first effort from a former insider who was in a unique position over a 25-year period to observe four CEOs develop and expand their understanding of a corporation's purpose and mission in our society. He also had contact with senior executives in other companies and industries during this period. It is bound to spark debate among corporate executives. For example, I recognize my understanding of the corporation's role in society in this chapter. However, other aspects of this chapter are new to me, and I am still comparing these ideas with my experience. But I believe this effort will result in a clearer understanding of the important role the corporation plays in our society.

Finally, I would like to commend the career path Ray Ewing has followed to other corporate management executives. After 35 years of experience as a professional manager in the business world, he chose to recareer into the academic field to help train future managers and to contribute to the management professions by writing, teaching, and consulting. Both the business community and society will benefit if more and more corporate executives use the later years of their careers in this manner. If qualified business leaders don't contribute to advance the knowledge base and the understanding of the business professions, who will?

Richard J. Haayen
Chairman and Chief Executive Officer
The Allstate Insurance Companies

CONTENTS

INTRODUCTION

Issues management is about power. It is about the power that controls the new bottom line of all American corporations— optimal profits *and* public acceptance.

It is about management of the legitimate power a corporation has over its total environment, when it is willing to use it. And it is about the power others have over the same environment and future of the corporation—power that can be shared through foresight and informed planning.

It is also about recovery of the power that has leaked out or been blown out of the center of management through the actions (or inactions) of internal and external agents.

Issues management emerged to fill this hole in the center of corporate management.

Issues management accomplishes this through a process that taps the collective wisdom of a corporation in a systematic, productive, and cost-effective manner.

Most CEOs readily acknowledge that wisdom in their corporations is not concentrated solely in the upper echelons, although some act as if it were. It is in fact distributed at all levels in the organization. The issues management process, when properly adapted to the management style and culture of a corporation, pulls together and concentrates this wisdom to focus on certain problems facing the corporation and to devise strategies to a-chieve a desired goal. It is also used to monitor the execution of those strategies.

Issues management is public policy foresight and planning for an organization. It is based on the concept that an organization is viable only if it has more influence over its environment than the environment has over it. Most corporate leaders now know that their corporations don't merely move in an economic arena but in a much larger sociopolitical environment that surrounds and controls success in the market place.

This new management technique is to corporate public policy/ public affairs planning and operations as strategic planning is to corporate business planning and operations. Issues management and strategic planning together give senior officers, especially CEOs, an enhanced capability to manage their enterprises in the present and the near-term future—1 to 3, 5, 10 or more years out.

The key to the development of both issues management and strategic planning is the consciously systematic effort to develop foresight based on present and past trends, forces, and anticipated changes. What is new about both processes in the practical world of corporate management is the deliberate effort to go beyond hunches and intuitive knowledge to develop a new type of knowledge—foreknowledge.

The strategic value of foreknowledge, no matter how sketchy or incomplete, is well known to every experienced executive. The reason is simple. Perceptive executives have learned one basic truth by the time they reach the leadership ranks of their organizations: Ignorance gets corporations into trouble; arrogance keeps them there.

Unfortunately, these executives fail to wring the full meaning from this truth after they finish the painful mopping-up exercises in the aftermath of their latest crisis. If they are to survive and advance both their careers and the interests of their employer, they go so far as to realize that they must be good crisis managers. But they too often stop there, without reflecting further.

If they paused to reflect further, they would know that the best executives of the future will be "pre-crisis" managers—and the top ones will be "no-crisis" managers. Every new CEO who utters that ancient corporate dictum to his staff, "No surprises!" in fact is signaling his desire to be a no-crisis manager. Unfortunately, few, if any, are ever able to overcome the inertia of institutional ignorance and arrogance and achieve that happy state.

The ignorance in question is management's lack of knowledge of what is going on in all the corporation's relevant environments, the social and political as well as the economic.

The arrogance is the unconscious arrogance of expertise when facing leaders who emerge from the sociomoral and political environments to challenge the actions of the corporation within its economic environment. "Not invented here"; "We know better what is good and safe for our customers than they or their advocates do"; "What is good for General Motors is good for . . ."; are common expressions of arrogance.

Automobile industry leaders displayed arrogance in the 1960s when they faced Ralph Nader and other unknowns who suddenly sprang up from "nowhere" as automobile safety advocates. The result was predictable: the clang of the iron cage of federal regulation dropping down, almost overnight, to constrain the entire industry for the first time in its history.

Ten years later, the banking and savings and loan industries had a similar encounter with the power of local community activists in metropolitan centers who accused them of redlining, refusing to grant loans in certain neighborhoods for homeownership and improvements. Because of a wrongheaded decision on the part of the financial institutions, the neighborhood action groups around the nation united and secured a federal law requiring banks and S&Ls to publicly disclose the amount of loans made to residents in the neighborhoods in which they were located, thereby leaving themselves open to depositor boycotts, regulatory complaints, and so on.

In the 1970s, the infant formula manufacturing and marketing industry reacted with ignorance and the arrogance of expertise to the highly publicized concerns of the religious, professional, and social constituencies that formed an activist coalition, INFACT. This industry suffered nearly a decade of abuse only to find in 1982 the constricting hand of the World Health Organization's Marketing Code close around its ability to sell its vital infant food supplement to developing countries. (Some advertising specialists call the WHO Code the "Non-marketing Code.") The leading manufacturer, Nestlé, which was singled out to "teach a lesson" to the other manufacturers, agonized through endless storms of public and governmental criticisms as it desperately strove to preserve its public reputation and its corporate self-respect within its employee family.

Many other examples will readily come to the mind of any seasoned executive. What is little understood is that these and other coercive regulatory "solutions" were not inevitable if the corporations involved had understood their total environment and the public policy process. Many nonlegislative paths to resolution of the basic issues in contention were open, except the status quo ante, which only the naive and insular executive believes is still open. But in order to see these paths and vigorously pursue them, senior management has to understand that it must decide to create its own future, rather than try to embalm the present.

An executive's first step in this process is to recognize that in our democracy society at large has the ultimate power to control any business or industry through the political process. Thus, social goals have an overriding power of priority when there is conflict between social goals and the economic goals of the business community, even though all social programs are ultimately paid for by money generated by the business community through the marketplace.

The social control of business is generally focused through the leadership of concerned citizens. And therein lie the dangers to unperceptive businessmen who do not completely understand their critics' basic rationales, motives, coalition power, and so on. Those dangers were best summarized by Supreme Court Justice Louis Brandeis who once wrote: "The greatest dangers to liberty lurk in the insidious encroachment by men of zeal, well-meaning but without understanding."

It is the responsibility of the business community to help such leaders acquire the necessary understanding when dealing with the free enterprise system or, failing that, to take their information to the interested publics—the power bases. This is a critical responsibility of the career executive, for in our society, corporations cannot long survive when their goals are perceived to be totally out of harmony with society's goals.

As the modern corporation has evolved, senior officers, especially CEOs, have come to understand the corporate role in our society. *They* have recognized for a number of years that despite the rhetoric and myths first formulated by Adam Smith two centuries ago, the modern business is not a single-purpose enterprise with the sole goal of *maximizing* profits for its owners, which in fact is impossible except for an absolute monopoly or a state-sponsored cartel, such as OPEC in the 1970s. They know that their corporations have many stakeholder groups—customers, employees, and the public in addition to the shareholders. The success and long-term viability of their corporations depend on the optimization of the satisfactions and expectations of all four stakeholder groups, not just those of the shareholders. That is the new bottom line of modern corporations, those that are prospering and will prosper and grow in the future. Profits still hold an essential position in the new bottom line, but success also demands that these profits be earned by satisfying the conditions for public acceptance.

However, in all societies there is always a cultural lag between the occurrence of a new insight or discovery and broader public understanding of its significance. Over the past several decades, senior corporate managers have noted the changing reality and the changing role society demands of their institutions. Many boards of directors have also reached this understanding, especially in the face of fierce national and global competition. Middle managers and the public at large are only now perceiving the change.

Issues management was developed within the business community as an educational task aimed at preserving the proper balance between the legitimate goals and rights of the free enterprise system and those of society. It is no historical accident that the appearance of democracies in the western world was accompanied by the industrial revolution. It is the responsibility of the business community leadership to preserve the public's understanding that economic justice is best won by free men and women through free enterprise—and to make sure the system delivers that result.

Created by Senior Management's Needs

The value of issues management to senior officers of major corporations has been attested to many times during the past several years. Here is what two experienced executives have said:

"The important issues don't just fade away. But those who don't manage them do."[1]

"Issues management is possibly the most important new management technique developed in the past two decades for the benefit of the chief executive officer."[2]

Issues management, considered a mere buzz word by indifferent management theorists and consultants but a few years ago, is now proving to be a new energizing force in the business community, where it originated. During the last several years, it has spread to the association, governmental, and academic worlds.

For example, Northwestern University's Kellogg Graduate School of Management in 1986 created the Institute for Health Issues Management. Its dynamic director, Professor Hilmon Sorey, Jr., selected the issues management process as the method to approach national health issue clusters, with public and private participation to develop future policy agendas at "surmising

---

[1]Frank J. Conner, president, American Can Company; speech before the Issues Management Association, New York, 1983.

[2]Donald F. Craib, Jr., chairman and CEO, Allstate Insurance Companies; speech before the Issues Management Association, Chicago, 1985.

forums." The deans of Kellogg and Northwestern's School of Law, Medical School, and Medill School of Journalism, recognizing the interdisciplinary nature of health issues management, have assigned senior academic staff members to the institute's Faculty Advisory Committee. They also participate in the institute's conferences. Karl D. Bays, chairman of Baxter Travenol Laboratories, chairs the institute's board.

President Reagan's creation of seven cabinet councils in 1982 to analyze various issue clusters and recommend policy for his cabinet's consideration is viewed as a form of issues management by Dr. Ralph Bledsoe, special assistant to the president and an executive secretary of one of the cabinet councils.

Thus, the issues management technique that emerged in the business sector has spread to other institutions under various guises. However, it is important to realize that this management process was an ad hoc development and not a theoretical invention.

If issues management was not invented in one creative burst, how did it come into being? It *evolved* to overcome a serious corporate weakness most senior officers became acutely aware of in the 1960s and 1970s. They learned a simple lesson the hard way: Ignorance gets corporations, like people, into trouble; arrogance keeps them there.

If ignorance gets corporations into trouble, then the development of foresight and understanding as to their external and internal environments, acted on with thoughtful planning and implementation, will keep them out of it. If arrogance keeps them mired in trouble when they fall into contention with external forces, then a responsible determination to work with other elements of society to resolve an issue will help them get out of real or avoid potential disasters. These realizations led to the gradual development of the issues management process by the public relations/public affairs staffs of sensitized corporations.

For "sensitized corporations," read sensitized CEOs, who found themselves increasingly embattled before congressional hearings, batteries of investigative reporters, and small armies of militant and demanding citizen groups. Attacks on business institutions increased in intensity as the black civil and economics rights revolution matured in the 1960s. The civil rights movement was joined by the consumer rights movement that expanded in the 1970s, and it in turn was joined by the women's rights and the youth revolutions. Confused corporate executives found themselves dragged into the public forums only to be charged and pilloried in ways never conceived of during the previous 200 years of American history.

They found that private business is no longer "private" in the sense that word was interpreted in the first half of this century.

Thus, corporate chief executives who had seldom spent more than 5 percent of their time on external affairs suddenly found themselves devoting 50 to 90 percent of their time on these matters. They became concerned with their companies' lack of understanding of and preparation for these encounters—and began telling their staffs this in sometimes colorful terms. Even then, they did not realize that there was a large, gaping hole in the middle of corporate management—the public policy management hole, a black hole that in turn adversely affected all profit management decisions and results.

I received the message from the then chairman of Allstate Insurance Companies, Judson B. Branch, following a stormy sequence of legislative hearings and encounters with consumerists challenging the insurance industry's underwriting and pricing practices in the late 1960s. After a particularly confusing and bitter exchange, Mr. Branch retreated to his office and summoned the general counsel and me, his public affairs director.

In a half-angry, half-humorous tone of voice, he told us, "Dammit, there *must* be a way of getting ahead of these developments!" I explained that there were scanning and forecasting techniques available and that I was already using some of them. I pointed to a memorandum supported by newsclips and other information I had sent to him several weeks earlier anticipating the consumerists' expanding their targets from the automobile industry to the insurance industry.

"How do you know I read them?" was his deflating response. Hotly, I replied that I carefully screened this kind of information and sent him only the most important and potentially significant material. "Naturally, because I flag it for your attention, I assume you read it," I concluded.

His response shocked me but seemed reasonable upon reflection. It was, "You cannot assume that I will read this kind of material. I am running a $3 billion company. The paper work, financial planning, and operational problems I deal with every day absorb nearly all of my time. *You* figure out a way for me to keep up with these matters so I can make decisions before time runs out and I am left with no opportunity to make any decision for the benefit of this company."

Checking later with public relations/public affairs executives in other industries, I discovered that similar conversations were going on during this period in their companies, too.

My response to this challenge was instantaneous, if slightly impertinent. "If I can't count on you reading the carefully selected material I send you, then we will have to get you in a conference room periodically. I will present the material on overhead slides and orally report our estimate of their significance. Then, unless you close your eyes and stick your fingers in your ears, we will know you are up to speed on developments we find."

Fortunately for me, Mr. Branch, a stern-visaged and forceful leader, also had a sense of humor. He dismissed us with a grin, saying "Fit these meetings into my schedule every three to six weeks. It's got to be a better system than paper reports. At least I can ask questions and get at the reasoning involved."

By the early 1970s, the Chairman's News Briefing, as it was called, became Allstate's first effort at public policy planning.

The meeting followed a simple format: The CEO, General Counsel George H. Kline (who later went on to become the CEO of two other financial services companies), and Vice President for Public Affairs Robert Leys, now retired, were the only senior officers in attendance. As the public affairs director (Allstate had changed the PR department's name to Public Affairs to signify its expanded functions several years earlier), I presented and interpreted various trends and developments the general counsel's office or our department had uncovered. Mr. Branch then questioned various interpretations until satisfied as to the probability of the development of certain issues. Then followed a general discussion of the impact on Allstate and the industry, suitable policy positions that might be taken, and so on. Approximately 10 percent of the time was spent on reporting current matters, the remainder on trends and future opportunities or problems they might represent.

During one of these early meetings, after extensive analysis of the consumerist and public interest movements, Allstate formulated its public advocacy role. Despite conventional wisdom then prevailing among many corporate executives that "self-appointed" consumer advocates had no legitimate standing (and should not be given any), our analysis convinced us that the First Amendment and the history of social movements legitimated their movements, if not some of their methods. In fact, it was obvious that in our democracy *anyone* had the right to champion any group or class of citizens or institutions.

This raised the question of the corporation's role. It became obvious that it had the right to become its *customers'* advocate in public matters, especially where there was a clear identity of interest in a public issue. Good management practices and enlightened self-interest clearly supported such a role. On the other hand, a more complex ethical issue emerged. What was the corporation's role when it acquired valid information of developments that extracted a penalty or worked to the detriment of its customers, who would fight to change or correct them if they had the knowledge and the ability to do so? Mr. Branch concluded that the corporation had the duty to serve as its customers' advocate in both cases.

From this decision flowed Allstate's leadership in developing national programs supported by advocacy advertising, beginning in the early 1970s. They included a program that got implied consent laws in those states without them (following the Department of Transportation's report to Congress showing that half of automobile fatalities involved a drunk driver). Other advocacy advertising programs involved getting better bumpers on cars to decrease unnecessary losses in low-speed accidents and urging adoption of the federal passive restraint (air bag) standard to eliminate unnecessary deaths and serious injuries in high-speed crashes. Although Allstate's enlightened self-interest was obvious in these campaigns, it proved its good faith by offering in advance 10 to 20 percent premium discounts on the relevant insurance coverages.

Two things should be noted in connection with Allstate's public policy decision: For the first time in American business history, the bumper and air bag campaigns pitted one industry (insurance) against another industry (automobile manufacturing) in a public policy fight; and for the first time, a major corporation built coalitions with public interest advocates (such as Ralph

Nader and the Center for Auto Safety) on these issues, with all members of the coalitions understanding that we were in agreement *only* on *this* issue and that we would probably be opposing each other on other public issues related to the conduct of business operations.

During this period, Allstate was not the only company and insurance was not the only industry that was in the process of rethinking its responsibilities in regard to public policy matters. Similar discussions and decisions were going on at the senior management level in other companies. In the insurance industry, State Farm, Travelers, Aetna, St. Paul, and John Hancock were among the early companies to develop their own public policy initiatives and strategies. Companies in other industries include W. R. Grace, Monsanto, Shell, Dow and, the most fiercely aggressive, Mobil, to name a few.

Thus, in the late 1960s and early 1970s, public relations/public affairs executives in between 15 to 20 companies were at work trying to fill the public policy hole in the center of senior corporate management planning. Each of us adapted foresight tools from think tanks, long-range planning (strategic planning) systems, and the social sciences. We did not do this as a conscious effort to create or invent a new management technique—we did it to meet our companies' needs. We also did it at the same time we were meeting our daily management responsibilities on behalf of our companies.

Like all valuable new management techniques, practice developed and outran university business school theory, which accounted for the bemused and sceptical attitudes of business schools when they first encountered our efforts. After all, hadn't they been preaching the concept of "corporate social responsibility" to hapless CEOs since the early 1920s? Unfortunately, they had never really advanced this concept beyond moralizing sermons that most post-World War II executives had already figured out for themselves.

Although the handful of corporate public relations professionals working on this new approach was developing scanning and forecasting techniques for their companies in the early 1970s, we rarely sat down together and discussed how we were doing it. We had no name yet for the process we were trying to develop. Some of us joined the World Future Society, where technical and scientific methods for social trends forecasting were demonstrated and debated by academics and utopians. The invasion of this society by 20 to 30 of us from the business community was first looked upon with suspicion. But by the mid-1970s, forecasters from the professional think tanks began to discuss our needs and debate alternative approaches with us.

Until that period, almost all corporate planning was primarily structured around senior managers' belief that the only planning they should be concerned with was their internal planning for their own business future. They mistakenly believed that the corporation had near absolute power over its own future so long as it could meet and beat the competition. This is the real reason why the public policy planning hole in corporate management existed for so long; CEOs believed that their government relations officers were sufficiently talented to block legislative and regulatory "interference" with their business on an ad hoc basis.

By the early 1970s, some business leaders began to realize that the "occasional" flurries of interference from citizen groups, academic activists, and politicians were not merely random, short-lived annoyances that had to be tolerated while they got on with the "real" business of future capital needs and market planning. They saw that their corporations were not only embedded in the economic environment, but also in the larger sociopolitical environment that has an equal power to control the eventual viability of the corporation.

In response, those leaders added "environmental analysis" to their tool kits and changed the name of long-range planning to strategic planning. However, in the offices of many CEOs it became clear that a separate planning process had to be developed for the sociopolitical environment, with expertise drawn from the public relations/public affairs professions. Those executives began to take another look at their slowly formalizing public policy foresight techniques and to consider seriously establishing a planning system.

At this juncture, a veteran corporate and governmental public relations/public affairs executive, W. Howard Chase, not only gave CEOs and other public relations professionals a name for the new process—"issues management"—in 1976, but also went on to develop the basic issues management process model in 1978. Chase's efforts catalyzed the subsequent rapid development of this management process, for each of us used his theory to reorganize our techniques and methods into a more powerful tool. In this sense, most corporate practitioners acknowledge Chase as the father of issues management, which without doubt he is.

Through Chase's efforts in publishing the *Corporate Public Issues* newsletter and in speaking and networking with other professionals, the public policy foresight and planning concept spread beyond the 15 to 20 corporate executives working on the technique to the majority of public relations and public affairs practitioners.

In 1977, the Public Affairs Council, whose members include the top corporations in America, took up the load and, through a series of national workshops over the next five years, performed the critical role of innovation. These workshops inspired hundreds of corporate executives to introduce the issues management process into their companies.

In 1978, Allstate's then chairman and chief executive officer, Archie R. Boe, decided that it was now time to formalize the company's public policy planning process. His executive committee had assumed policy making functions, but the turbulent economic situation at the time forced this committee to become immersed in operating decisions. Corporate Relations Vice President Larry H. Williford and I had become concerned that individual departments were, in effect, making public policy decisions for the whole company without sufficient discussions with other affected departments. Williford made our concern known to Boe, and he asked for recommendations. I drew up an issues management system based on my knowledge of what we had done in the past, current thinking as reflected by Chase's process model, and the corporate culture inside Allstate. My plan was expanded from the department officer level to the senior officer level by Williford and Boe. Executive Vice President Richard J. Haayen and I developed the final operating procedures for the system.

In 1977, Boe had expanded Allstate's traditional long-range *business* planning process and had formed a senior officer Strategic Planning Committee to direct it. Now he created a senior officer policy making committee, the Issues Management Committee. At the same time, he appointed me issues management director and secretary of the Issues Management Committee. The senior officer committee was first chaired by Vice Chairman

Donald S. Craib, Jr., who became Allstate's chairman and CEO four years later.

When I contacted Chase and his associate, Barry Jones, to get the names of other full-time corporate issues management staff leaders, they informed me that I was the first corporate executive to get the title and Boe was the first CEO to create a formal senior officer issues management committee. He then welcomed me into the hardy band of issues management pioneers!

Chase, Vice President Raymond Hoewing of the Public Affairs Council, and I each became national network centers for persons interested in the issues management process. Because of the burden of daily telephone calls, correspondence, and so forth, Chase and I decided to form the Issues Management Association to get all the practitioners from different disciplines (such as public relations, law, economics, and the social sciences) under one tent and let members talk to each other. *The Wall Street Journal* mentioned our intention at the bottom of a front-page column on August 25, 1981, and every day over the next two weeks, we were inundated with hundreds of phone calls and letters. Margaret Stroup, Monsanto's new issues management director, was mentioned in the same column. She also had to enlist staff to help answer telephone calls and handle the mail—cleverly referring inquiries to Chase and me.

Chase and I each invited 10 practitioners to the Harvard Club of New York to join us as cofounders of the Issues Management Association in December 1981. Chase was elected acting chairman of the board, and I was elected acting president. I arranged for the first meeting of the association at the Library of Congress, through fellow cofounder Walter Hahn early in March 1982.

Although only 100 letters were sent out over my signature to major corporations and consultants who had contacted Chase and me earlier, we had 104 fully paid members by the time the founding membership meeting opened. Other than the first 100 letters sent out, we had no membership recruitment program during IMA's first four months. Yet membership grew to 400 by August of 1982, and I moved the association's files out of my secretary's desk to the association's hastily created headquarters Chase had arranged for in Stamford, Connecticut. Thus, by the end of 1982 issues management as a new management discipline was formally established. Since then, colleges and universities have begun to teach courses in this new technique, consulting firms have added it to their arsenal, and new developments and enrichment of Chase's process model now occur almost monthly.

Today, most of the nation's top 2,000 corporations have some formal issues management process in place somewhere in the corporate structure (although it may be buried under such names as public policy research, public issues, or public affairs planning, and bootlegged into one department rather than placed at the senior management level).

The above account dwells on Allstate's experience for two reasons. First, I was personally involved in its emergence over a 16-year period and am familiar with senior management's thinking in regard to issues management. Second, Boe's decision to make senior officers responsible for issues management rather than placing it in one department not only accounted for Allstate's successful integration of the process into the company's decision making process; Boe's matrix senior officer Issues Management Committee also served as an early model for other large companies.

In addition, since I was the first identifiable corporate executive with an issues management title, hundreds of managers and officers from large and small corporations contacted me from 1978 onward as to how to set up a process in their companies. The successes and failures are familiar to me, as are the reasons for both, which will be discussed later in this book.

So far the discussion has focused on CEOs internalizing the issues management process in the daily management of their companies.

From the early 1960s on, considerable pressure was brought against corporate boards of directors as a result of the changing American social, political, and economic environments. Many CEOs decided to respond by creating board committees under such titles as Public Policy Committee and Public Issues Committee, with heavy membership of outside directors. The CEOs usually appointed themselves to these committees, plus one other officer, usually their chief operating officer.

The staff work for these board committees was and is usually assigned to one department—such as public relations or public affairs. Two notable examples are the Bank of America and Sears, Roebuck and Company.

The late James Langton, Bank of America's veteran public relations vice president, was the officer responsible for the staff work for the board committee. He once explained privately to me the advantages and especially the disadvantages of this type of issues management system, when a parallel issues management system is not created within the company.

The major disadvantage, Langton told me, was primarily that the system had only an indirect influence on the company's internal management. The public relations department and especially his unit were perceived internally as responsible for issues management—and then only for the board, not for the operating management decisions, even though they had an internal officer policy committee. The other departments felt that BOA's CEO would pass on to them any policy decisions or directions; otherwise they didn't consider Langton's operation relevant to them. In fact, Langton told me he faced the usual territorial barriers when he tried to get certain information, estimates, and so on from other departments. Only his skill, developed earlier as the bank's public relations officer, served him in wheedling the necessary information from reluctant department heads.

He thought Boe's senior management matrix Issues Management Committee, which included the officers responsible for all of Allstate's line and staff operations, was superior. This was because I faced no territorial defensive resistance from department officers in seeking data or department personnel to work on issue subcommittees, mainly because the department officer's immediate superior, or his boss's immediate superior, sat on the issues committee. Each department officer knew that his function was properly represented on the issues committee, and that the men responsible for his future career advancement sat on that committee. Therefore, each department officer was personally committed to the success of the company's issues management process. In addition, all were interested in learning from me how they could use the process to get the policy decisions they needed to run their departments. Langton told me that he was unable to establish that kind of relationship.

Instead, although he and his staff did brilliant issues analysis and foresight work, he said he had to threaten various departmental officers to get progress reports from them on board policy plans. His threat was simple: If he didn't get a report or if a department had made no progress on the board's policy recommendations, he would have to report that result at the next board meeting. Despite these difficulties, Langton was able to make the issues management process work at the senior management level.

The issues management system at Sears, Roebuck and Co. is also designed for a board of directors' committee. However, the staff analysis, reports, and recommendations under the direction of issues manager John Snow are presented not only to the board, but also to the headquarters department heads and to the planning officers of each of the Sears' groups—such as retail, insurance, and financial services.

CHAPTER TWO

Makes Strategic Management Possible

Issues management is not a complicated concept. It is simply *public policy* research, foresight, and planning for an organization in the private sector impacted by decisions made by others in the public sector. It is not totally absorbed with government relations issues or *public affairs* as that term is used in corporations to refer to the internal legislative and regulatory management function. Its reach and beneficial contributions extend beyond the corporate public affairs department operations.

Issues management fills the policy hole in the center of corporate management, making it possible for the CEO and senior management to strategically manage their enterprise as a whole, as a complete entity capable of helping create the future and "grow" their company into it. It also has the capability of checking operational projects in light of major corporate policy to make sure the corporation is functioning as an integrated whole, getting maximum results from company resources.

Strategic planning, with which issues management is frequently confused, is the other half of the planning platform on which CEOs and their senior staffs must stand to successfully guide their companies through the present and into the future.

Strategic planning is *business* (economic) research, foresight, and planning. Both issues management and strategic planning use similar techniques, share research, and reinforce each other in support of the organization's bottom line. Together, they give senior management the ability to strategically manage an enterprise with greater efficiency and effectiveness.

Borrowing from nautical terminology, strategic management is now possible because the CEO, as captain of the enterprise, has at his or her command a chief operating officer (COO), who serves as pilot, and the issues management and strategic planning staffers, who serve as navigators. Large and small enterprises founder because one of the three—captain, pilot, or navigator—is either not aboard or is derelict in duty.

Basic differences between the two planning processes exist. In 1978, under the leadership of Donald F. Craib, Jr., then chairman of Allstate's Issues Management Committee (and later vice chairman of Sears, Roebuck and Co. before becoming Allstate's CEO), the following differences were identified and used as guides by senior management and staff.

Issues Management (concerned with or can effect)	Strategic Planning (concerned with or can effect)
Outside planning in	Inside planning out
Issues 1−3 years out in future	Issues 1−5 + years out in future
Operational (annual) plans	Organizational (long-range) plans
Defense/opportunity	Opportunity/defense
Best of contentious bargain	Best of self-created bargain

Under this construct, it can be seen that issues management is concerned with (1) plans that groups outside an organization are making in the sociopolitical and economic environment (the public policy process) that would impact the corporation's future, and, (2) the outside plans the corporation must make for itself as it seeks to participate in the public policy process.

Thus, it is a recognition that others (such as public activists, politicians, competitors, regulators, and would-be regulators) outside the corporation are planning the corporation's future on their terms. Issues management's goal is to intervene consciously and effectively and participate early in the process, instead of waiting passively until the organization finds itself a victim at the tail end of the process. The corporation seeks viability—it seeks to have more influence over its environment than the environment has over it.

Strategic planning, on the other hand, is primarily concerned with the corporation's internal planning for its own business (economic) future. Until the last decade, most senior officers mistakenly believed that the corporation had near absolute power over its own future, so long as it could meet and beat the competition in the marketplace. However, the marketplace is and was never solely an economic arena, but is regulated by the political power and legitimated by the sociomoral power of the public, which, as I pointed out, business leaders began to realize in the early 1970s.

On the issues time frame, issues management is concerned with issues that will begin to move, mature, or be resolved 12 months to 3 years in the future. Thus, issues managers seldom (and should not) work on issues that are being resolved in the current year. Company policy and plans already exist, by the force of circumstances and functional departments' normal operating procedures.

Many companies with an issues management process in place fall into the error of turning it into a crisis management tool to deal with current operational problems. Additionally, an issues management system incurs unnecessary resistance from functional departments if it is used as a method to interfere on a weekly basis with public affairs, marketing, and other staffs that are in the field trying to resolve current issues and problems. This prevents the issues management staff from performing its real duties, developing foreknowledge and plans for the future. If the issues management system has been in place for a year, it should have developed policy and plans for guidance for the current year. Current matters can be referred to it quickly, but only for clarification and evaluation of ongoing results.

However, senior management must guard against departmental officers' and group officers' understandable efforts to shift their responsibilities for execution of company policy to the group decisions made in the issues management system. Management discipline is eroded if this is permitted to occur because when everybody is responsible, no one is accountable for results in the operating arena.

If issues management is locked into current crisis management problems, it has failed as a pre-crisis or a no-crisis planning system. If everyone in the company is busy bailing out the boat or manning the pumps, no one is looking for the nearest port or safe landfall. The company has wasted its time and money setting up the issues management system.

There are two reasons why the issues time frame is one to three years out (years two through four from the present). The first is psychological: Most CEOs today have an average tenure of about five years. The CEO is strictly accountable in fact only for his or her years of leadership, despite talk and theory to the contrary. Consequently, the CEO's attention is sharply focused on those years, recognizing that future issues are the responsibility of the succeeding CEO. Natually the current CEO wants a system that will help the next CEO navigate, which in fact is what the issues management and strategic planning processes provide. However, the current CEO wants only current issues on his plate. Normal scanning and monitoring work of the issues management staff reaches out and identifies issues that go many years into the future, but the temperament of the CEO determines that only the nearer-term issues will be brought before senior management for policy making.

The second reason for the issues time frame is this: It is the time frame in which public issues reach their climax phase, when their velocity reaches maximum peak. As will be discussed later, the life cycle of an issue on the national level is roughly between 6 and 12 years. In many of those years, it appears dead or dormant only to rise and move rapidly to resolution sometime within a 12- to 18-month climax period.

Because of this shorter time frame, issues management planning is primarily restricted to adjustments in the current operations of a company.

On the other hand, strategic planning can operate in the longer-term future, which gives ample time to consider and develop plans for complex organizational changes needed to expand or move into new businesses or industries. Thus, longer-term issues that the issues management process identifies are usually referred to the strategic planners who, after preliminary policy implications are considered, can factor them into their more comprehensive organizational planning process.

This last difference relates to the corporate purposes of the two planning processes. Issues management's first responsibility is to make sure that the corporation is defended against whatever tactic the legions of organized and unorganized actors in the public policy forum mount. This role is in response to the fierce dictum each new generation of CEOs lays on the management staff: "No surprises!"

Issues management's second responsibility is to seek out and identify opportunities inherent in the issues others generate or *the company seeks to generate.*

Strategic planning, on the other hand, concentrates on the exploitation of corporate business opportunities, with a secondary responsibility for contingency planning to protect against competitive reversals, economic discontinuities, and so on.

Thus, issues management seeks to gain the best results out of a contentious bargain others try to create; strategic planning seeks the best results out of a good bargain the corporation creates.

The potential of these two planning processes, working in tandem, was pointed out by Boe in 1979: "Issues management and strategic planning are both born of the dynamic tradition in American business management that rejects the passive approach of hoping to know the future and merely adjusting to it, for an affirmative posture of *creating* the future and *fitting* the corporate enterprise into it."[1]

ISSUES MANAGEMENT IS NOT . . .

At this point it would be useful to understand what issues management is not. Issues management is *not* management of issues through the public policy forums in our democracy or management of the public policy process itself. ("Management" is used here in its normal usage in the business world: the ability to significantly control and direct.)

Not even the most powerful chief executive in the world, the president of the United States, can or ever has been able to accomplish that in our democracy. One need but try to recall even one major issue Nixon, Ford, Carter, or Reagan really "managed" through the national public policy forums in this country, despite

---

[1]A. R. Boe, "Fitting the Corporation to the Future," *Public Relations Quarterly*, Winter 1979, pp. 4–5.

their protestations to the contrary, to realize the impossibility of the task. In fact, the U.S. Constitution and its amendments are designed to prevent anyone from accomplishing this, for which we can all thankfully say, "Amen!"

Issues management is the management of an institution's resources and efforts to *participate* in the successful resolution of issues in our public policy process.

The reader should be aware that a minority of issues management consultants seem to claim in their presentations to potential clients that, with their help, the client could manage and significantly steer an issue through the public forums in our society. However, in private conversation with this author, most of them admit that they really mean management of the client's resources and efforts, The one or two who seem to be arguing to the contrary take "management" as their goal, but they are veterans of the pre-1950s' legislative-regulatory-business power structure world, which no longer exists. So-called successes during that period were, in fact, only partial and usually short lived.

MISSION STATEMENT: ISSUE FRAMER

The modern corporation began to redefine itself significantly in the 1970s, as noted earlier. However, the sweeping significance of this change has not been looked at from an historically objective standpoint.

The change began to formalize as the corporate planning concept moved from the pre-World War II short-term planning and control through the annual budgeting process. Following World War II, the military concept of long-range planning (a rolling five-year plan) was adopted in the corporate world. However, it was primarily numbers (financial) planning. As society's standards for business conduct changed, this form of planning was inadequate. Until this change occurred, classic economic theory prevailed—the purpose of an enterprise was primarily to maximize profits for the benefit of the owners (shareholders).

However, a broadly educated public and public interest advocates began to challenge the purpose of a corporation beyond price, product, and profits for the owners. The public began to examine corporate social behavior, corporate social responsibility, and corporate citizenship.

The development of strategic planning as a new process, which moved beyond numbers planning to take into account social and business trends and other environmental factors, was the first major response to the changing demands society placed on corporations.

Early in the development of strategic planning theory and techniques, SRI International devised a strategic planning system that literally hung from what was described as the corporate "mission statement." The mission statement is management's formulation of the corporation's purposes, the charter the corporation and management operates under. Previously, a corporation's articles of incorporation, which details the lines of business it may engage in, guided senior management but was seldom elaborated on for all corporate employees. The founder or an outstanding CEO might have or might develop a vision for the corporation in which its goals and standards were clearly stated. But these goals were usually not developed beyond a motto for lower management and employees.

As public and political pressure mounted in the effort to force corporations to achieve some of the nation's social goals, CEOs began to develop codes of ethics or corporate principles. However, it was not until strategic planning was seriously integrated into management's guidance system that a comprehensive look was taken at such questions as What business are we in? Who do we really serve? Who is invested in our enterprise beyond the shareholders?

The mission statement attempts to answer this. It identifies the company's purpose and goals in relation to newly recognized constituencies beyond the owners. These formally recognized constituencies are called "stakeholders" in developing the mission statement. All mission statements recognize the company's primary stakeholders as customers, employees, the general public, and shareholders.

Only after the mission statement is created, identifying the purpose, goals, and stakeholders, can a comprehensive corporate plan be created and refined. Thus, the stakeholders identified in the mission statement and the company's commitment to serve the legitimate interest of each determine the universe within which planning may be done.

For the issues management staff, the issues scanned for and monitored are those that might have significant impact on the company's stakeholders and, hence, the company's future.

Before continuing, the *modern* corporate form of enterprise should be examined. The next section represents this author's attempt to describe it. The description is based on the vantage point of spending 35 years inside several corporate headquarters observing the changes occurring and discussing these changes with CEOs and planners who were formalizing them in their companies.

CHAPTER THREE

The Evolution of the Modern Corporation and Its Mission

The prevailing economic theory of any business enterprise, including the publicly held corporation, is that it exists solely and primarily for the *maximization* of profits for its owners. This concept goes back to the first modern economist—Adam Smith. And until the mid-1930s, American courts always affirmed this theory. For example, when Henry Ford sought to divert earnings of the Ford Motor Company to the improvement of employees' living conditions early in this century, the courts ruled he could not do it. The earnings belonged to the stockholders, as the stockholder-plaintiffs asserted.

However, pressures began building in American society early in this century with the elaboration of antitrust laws and other business regulations protecting the consumer and society. A gradual threat began to form: Either business should redefine itself in terms of its total environment, or society through its control of elected officials would do it.

For example, when the 1936 Internal Revenue Code was passed, corporations could for the first time take charitable contribution deductions if the contributions were *not* for business purposes but were for the betterment of economic and social conditions. Previously, businesses could take only a *business* deduction for charitable contributions and only if the contribution directly furthered the interests of the business. They were not permitted to take a "charitable" contribution deduction, based on the theory that businesses—especially corporations—existed for the maximization of profits for the stockholders. Stockholders, the theory went, could if they wished support the charities of their choice when they received their dividends, but the corporation itself could not. Even after passage of the 1936 IRS Code, the University of Chicago School—led by the late Frank Knight earlier in this century and by his pupil Milton Friedman today—vigorously defended this rule. Knight argued that a business was a purely economic institution and in no sense ever a social institution. Reflection and the expanded view of the times have eroded this extreme, 19th-century view.

The modern view is best expressed by Peter F. Drucker, the one man who has spent more than 50 years studying at first hand the American corporation and its management.

To illustrate the shift, Drucker in *Management: Tasks, Responsibilities, Practices* cites a contemporary economist, Joel Dean. Dean has written: "Economic theory makes a fundamental assumption that maximization of profits is the basic objective of every firm. But in recent years, profit maximization has been extensively qualified by theorists to refer to the long run; to refer to managements' rather than the owners' income; . . ." Dean goes on to write: "This trend reflects a growing realization by theorists that many firms, and particularly big ones, do not operate on the principle of profit maximization in terms of marginal costs and revenues. . . ."[1]

Discussing Dean's observations Drucker states: "A theorem that can be maintained only when qualified out of existence has surely ceased to have meaning or usefulness." Drucker argues that "profitability is not the purpose of but a limiting factor on business enterprises and business activities. Profit is not the explanation, cause or rationale of business behavior and business decisions, but the test of their validity."[2]

It is this persistent profit maximization misconception of the role of the corporation, he says, that causes the public to view the business community with hostility. They believe that there is an inherent contradiction between maximum profit-seeking and a

---

[1]As cited in P. F. Drucker, *Management: Tasks, Responsibilities, and Practices* (New York: Harper & Row, 1974).

[2]Ibid., pp. 59–60.

company's ability to make social contributions. Taking Drucker's reasoning one step further, the profit maximization goal in theory would cause a business or corporation to seek maximum profit from each sale, i.e., seek to pauperize each customer by extracting as much as possible in the exchange, limited only by the customer's personal wealth. Thus, the greater the success of the business, the greater the eventual loss of impoverished customers. Eventually, the profit maximizer would run out of its customer base, for that is always finite.

On the other hand, Drucker argues that "a company can make a social contribution only if it is highly profitable."[3] But, he says, that is not the purpose of a business as an economic process. The corporation has only one purpose according to him: to create customers.[4]

Markets are created by businessmen and women, not by economic forces, trends, or mysterious economic laws. Customers' wants are merely potential demands until the action of a business organization converts them into effective demands. No one, Drucker says, knew he wanted a telephone, a photocopying machine, or a computer until they were created and made available. These businesses created their own customers.

Thus, although he displaces the maximization of profit as the central and only purpose of a modern corporation, Drucker argues that profit is the essential socioeconomic result that a business must generate as a by-product of its main purpose: the creation of customers. Therefore, he states, business managers should never apologize for earning profits, but for *not* earning them, for they have not only failed the owners, the employees, and the customers, but society as a whole. His argument is that profit is more crucial for society than it is for the individual business. Why? Because all social and governmental programs are funded in the end by profits from the marketplace—a society sinks to a mere subsistence level of existence without the wealth-producing and accumulating activities of successful businesses.

If the profit maximization theory is immoral, as Drucker argues, what legitimates the modern corporation—what is our current understanding of the moral base of the corporation? His

---

[3]Ibid., p. 60.
[4]Ibid., p. 61.

answer: "We long ago learned that it is the job of the business manager to convert public needs into business opportunities." He argues further for the justification of management authority, "It is the purpose of organization and, therefore, the grounds of management authority to make human strength productive." The invention of the business (corporate)form of organization to accomplish social purposes in his view is one of the most important discoveries in human history. In reality it represents the principle not that "private vices make public benefits," but that "personal strengths make social benefits."[5]

Thus, the moral justification of the free enterprise system and managerial autonomy is that managers, while private, know themselves to be public men and women, responsible for their own specific duties in helping advance the quality of life in society.

What evidence exists to support this view of the evolution of the modern corporation? How did we get from the 19th-century concept of the corporation as purely an economic profit maximizer to today's corporation where CEOs can, with confidence, say: "More than ever, corporations are social institutions, with talents and resources that can be used in support of social objectives."[6]

We need but look to the development of the central business planning concepts since World War II. More than anything, the planning systems used by corporations reflect senior managements' understanding of the purpose of their companies and their responsibilities to them.

Prior to World War II, corporate planning consisted primarily of developing the next year's budget. It was a production/sales, costs/profits projection. Any longer-term planning was done sporadically and on an ad hoc basis by the CEO when circumstances or a personal sense of responsibility so moved him.

By the 1950s, the concept of long-range (five-year) planning was slowly adopted from the military, because most of the CEOs had become familiar with the concept during their service in the war. However, this was still numbers planning, costs/profits. When the nation adopted a social agenda in the 1960s, making

---

[5]Ibid., p. 810.

[6]John H. Bryan, Jr., chairman Sara Lee Corporation, quoted in *Chicago Magazine*, October 1986, p. 165.

enormous demands on the business community, the need for a new type of planning was recognized. From this need, the concept of strategic planning (the terminology again borrowed from the military) emerged in the 1970s—going beyond numbers planning, including socioeconomic environmental factors, and for the first time including the recognition of other stakeholders beyond the usual stockholders/customers.

At the same time business planning evolved to its present level of comprehensiveness, public policy planning for corporations emerged in the 1970s to meet the recognized needs of the changing public role of business entities in our society. These two planning processes, strategic planning and issues management, thus gave senior management for the first time the ability to strategically manage their corporations and legitimate privately owned enterprises in our free enterprise system.

Since most veteran business executives have long recognized that the concept of the corporation has changed over the past two decades, we need to define or describe the modern corporation in new terms. We need to look at it systemically, as an organic whole, with its own purposes, energy, and function. What follows is my attempt to describe the currently evolved status of the modern corporation. There exist many models, definitions, and descriptions of corporations, but they were usually constructed for specific purposes—financial, marketing, and so forth. This description has the purpose of trying to understand the corporation as a whole, one to which all functions in the corporation can be related.

THE CORPORATION

"It is the job of the business manager to convert public needs into business opportunities" (Peter F. Drucker).[7]

"All business in a democracy begins with public permission and exists by public approval" (Arthur W. Page, former AT&T executive).[8]

---

[7]Ibid.

[8]"The Page Philosophy," Arthur W. Page Society, Chicago, 1985.

It is startling to discover how little contemporary business leaders understand the legal basis for the existence of an enterprise. There is nothing in the U.S. Constitution or its amendments that guarantees the rights of free enterprise institutions to exist in the same sense that the rights of citizens are guaranteed. The federal and state laws that govern the creation and operation of businesses are just that—laws—which can be amended or revoked in any session by the legislatures to reflect the will of the public. It can be truly said that businesses exist by public approval, and not only because the public can vote with its pocketbook by refusing to patronize a commercial enterprise. It can also vote with its ballots to elect those legislators who will pass laws to eliminate or prohibit certain businesses or business practices.

The corporation is the most efficient and effective form of organization for medium- and large-scale business enterprises, benefiting from *economies of scale* in capital formation, technology, production, management, marketing, public relations, and stakeholder satisfactions.

An economic historian has pointed out that the corporation is one of the "great surprises" of Western civilization, primarily because it led to the discovery of economies of scale. The private wealth of individuals or families was not sufficient to capitalize the great commercial projects needed at certain stages of social development, especially after the mass consumer markets emerged in successful nations. As public offerings were made and the limited liability corporation emerged, the professional managers of the corporations discovered that by increasing investments in all factors at the same time to the same degree, a quantum leap in results occurred. That is, when they tripled all inputs, output was more than tripled. Enterprises of scale also favorably impacted humans, creating great pools of skilled labor in communities where previously none existed. These labor pools attracted other enterprises to the communities. New technologies of scale emerged to meet the new opportunities. Thus, despite persistent criticisms by populists, the energy of the great corporations of scale over time succeeded in helping raise about 80 percent of American families into the middle class by the late 1960s—as sociologist Daniel Bell has pointed out, a feat no other society ever before accomplished.

A corporation exists for the *optimization* of the satisfactions of its stakeholders.

Once corporate leaders began to acknowledge they had more than one group of stakeholders, i.e., their stockholders or shareholders, then the classical goal of maximization of the owners' profits went by the board. When you have two or more parties at interest, you cannot maximize one party's benefits without diminishing the other's. Instead, corporate leaders set out to optimize the benefits for all stakeholders, that is, secure the most favorable results for all parties under the circumstances.

Acknowledged stakeholders are recognized in a corporation's mission statement, which states the company's purpose and goals. These stakeholders, whether identified or not, may be divided into two basic groups:

> Primary: Customers
> Employees
> Shareholders
> General public

The adoption of the strategic planning method by almost every major corporation in the United States in the 1970s involved the creation of a company-specific mission statement, which identified the company's purposes, goals, stakeholders, and commitments to them. For the first time, corporations sought to understand and describe the major elements necessary for the success and viability of a going business concern as an open, self-regulating system.

As Drucker pointed out, objectively speaking the business enterprise exists because it creates and satisfies the needs of customers. However, it cannot create or service customer needs without an employee force, i.e., the work force is essential to the existence of an enterprise. Indeed, with the growth of knowledge-based industries, employees have become the "strategic resource" of every modern corporation, as John Naisbitt has pointed out in *Re-Inventing the Corporation*, replacing in primacy financial capital, machines, and other items formerly considered the only strategic resources. Employees are no longer viewed as an unavoidable cost of doing business, worthy of a mere subsistence wage as the 19th-century view held, but as a major strategic resource as relevant as the other resources a business depends on. Hence the contemporary recognition of their stake in the corporation.

The shareholders, being the owners of record of publicly held corporations, have always been viewed as a primary stakeholder of the business corporation. But today they are no longer viewed as the only stakeholder worthy of recognition. The shareholders' position is often misunderstood, especially by populists, who view shareholders as if they were the proprietors of the business. Adolph Berle in past decades and Ralph Nader in current times have aroused much concern over the alleged separation of "the incidences of ownership" from stockholders—that is, if you were the proprietor of a store or a professional office, you could use the facilities of the business as you wished, hold a party after hours for friends and neighbors, and so on. This is a disingenuous argument, for a sole proprietor is actively engaged in the ownership and operation of the business and is personally liable for all actions. The stockholder is a passive investor in an income-producing venture, with limited liability in regard to the business. His or her motives are not entrepreneurial, but those of a passive rentier, knowingly dependent on professional managers to conserve and manage the business. The stockholder is financially invested in the enterprise, not actively, professionally, or practically committed. Loyalty is dividend deep; shares will be sold if a better return can be found elsewhere. This is also true of the large institutional investors, who soon will own over 50 percent of our largest companies. But the viable corporation goes on. Shareholders are of paramount importance to the corporation, though, for they are not only the source of current capital, but of future capital for growth, expansion, and long-term profitability as well.

The shareholders' total returns must always approximate the risk of the passive investment involved. That is management's responsibility. But their self-interest rights do not completely override the interests of society and the other stakeholders in publicly held corporations.

The current crisis resulting from hostile takeovers, forced mergers, sell-offs, and cannibalization of assets through share-ownership control of publicly held corporations is based on the old ownership misconceptions still reflected in our laws. It permits investment specialists, not the producers of wealth, to garner short-term, legal, but unearned, windfalls to the detriment of all of the other corporate stakeholders. Congress will correct this, especially through the work of Rep. John D. Dingell's House Committee on Energy and Commerce, to see that all stakeholders' interests are protected from the depredations of a few irresponsible members of the financial community. Society is now in the process of balancing property rights with rights of membership.

The general public is not only the great pool from which customers, employees, and shareholders spring, but it controls the legitimacy of any business in its midst, either informally through custom and culture or formally as the electorate that in the end controls governmental actions.

> Secondary or Mediating: News Media
> Suppliers and/or dealers
> Financial markets
> Governments (local, state and federal)

Some companies, according to their lines of business, recognize other stakeholders. Unacknowledged or unrecognized stakeholders may exist or come into being based on a group's belief that it has a real or imagined vested interest in the corporation, e.g., public interest groups and minorities.

I use the term *mediating* to define these stakeholders (although current strategic planning literature does not) because they perform a mediating function between the corporation and its primary stakeholders. In addition, no mission statement I know of lists the news media as a stakeholder; however, this is an oversight because the media are essential not only to the marketing function of a corporation, but in communicating with all corporate stakeholders.

Line operations meet satisfaction needs of customers; staff supports line in meeting those needs and is responsible for meeting needs of the other corporate stakeholders.

The stakeholder concept has eroded the line-staff divisions inside the modern corporation. It is now more fashionable to refer to functional departments, which include all units serving one or more stakeholder groups.

Levels of stakeholder satisfactions can be empirically quantified.

Stakeholder satisfactions create a corporation's *goodwill*, the major intangible asset of a viable corporation, being the difference between the current market value of the entire firm and the sum of its net individual assets. Accountants also define goodwill as the future earnings potential of a corporation in excess of average earnings for companies in its industry.

Accountants have long given specific meaning to and used methods of evaluating a company's goodwill when it was purchased or sold. Yet in practice professional corporate managers have treated the concept as a nebulous, airy concept of little overall value in planning for and managing their enterprise. Not until the concept of the mission statement and the company's stakeholders emerged did the relationship of goodwill and specific publics, the stakeholders, begin to emerge.

Accounting Research Study No. 10, "Accounting for Goodwill," The American Institute of Certified Public Accountants, 1968, includes the following among its list of factors contributing to goodwill:

1. Superior management team
2. Outstanding sales manager or organizations
3. Effective advertising
4. Good labor relations
5. Outstanding credit rating resulting from an established reputation for integrity, providing a company extra equity "leverage"
6. Top-flight training program for employees
7. High standing in a community through contributions to charitable activities and participation in civic activities by company officers
8. Favorable tax conditions
9. Favorable government regulation

The study also points out that the views of investors are influenced by the public image of a company. "The image may have been created by the specific efforts and expenditures of the company, or may have resulted from other forces that mold most public opinion."[9] It is obvious that the traditional business ac-

---

[9]American Institute of Certified Public Accountants, "Accounting for Goodwill," *Accounting Research Study No. 10*, New York, 1968, p. 15.

counting for goodwill implied the existence of the primary stakeholder groups. However, management could not plan for and strive to improve its overall state of goodwill until the strategic planning and issues management tools were forged.

Negative goodwill is also a term of art in the world of business, being the difference between the lower market value of a going business enterprise and the higher value of the sum of its tangible assets.

Goodwill is *earned* by the corporation through its performance. It is stabilized and enhanced by professionally managed communications, but cannot be created by communications alone (unless the corporation is in the communications business).

Goodwill is manifested through public opinion, or the opinions of a corporation's stakeholder publics. In this sense a corporation's viability and legitimacy rests on public opinion, rather than law.

Although accountants record goodwill only when a company is bought, management has many methods of checking on the level of its company's goodwill. The price/earnings ratio of the company's shares in the daily stock market, customer satisfaction levels in market tracking studies, employee morale surveys, and stockholder surveys are a few of the many methods available.

The chief executive officer (CEO) is accountable to the board of directors, representing the corporation's owners (shareholders), for the overall performance of the corporation, including the state of its goodwill, which significantly relates to the total market value of the enterprise.

From this description, the role of each functional department—production, marketing, and so on—can be determined, if the corporation is to operate and focus on its mission and goals. Below is a description of one of the least understood functions in the modern corporation.

THE PUBLIC RELATIONS FUNCTION

The public relations department is accountable to the CEO as the staff unit primarily responsible for management of the corporation's communications with its stakeholders, except for those communication tasks inherent in and integral to other departments' execution of their functions. However, even then, the public relations unit has the responsibility to be available as a staff resource to those departments. Its overall duty is to professionally communicate the corporation's performance and achievements in serving the needs of its primary stakeholders.

Issues Management

From the above description of the integrated system that a modern corporation represents, we can better understand its role in the public policy process it lives in. That senior managers recognize this is beyond question, although lower management ranks may not have reached this level of insight due to their narrowly focused responsibilities within the corporation. One need but consider this statement by Robert O. Anderson in 1982 when he was chairman and CEO of the Atlantic Richfield Company:

> After 20 years of debate, discussion, and confrontation, it's the rare chief executive officer who is not concerned with his company's public affairs program, who does not understand that the attitudes of employees, consumers, shareholders, government, the press, and the public in general have infinitely important consequences for business. This is the theater of public affairs. As we have seen repeatedly demonstrated in recent years, failure to perform competently and creditably in this realm can be devastating to the prospects of any business. In fact, it's not stretching fact at all to say that *business today has a new "bottom line"—public acceptance.* Without the approval and support of society, it's obvious that financial success is irrelevant. [Emphasis added.][10]

---

[10]J. S. Nagelschmidt, ed., *The Public Affairs Handbook* (New York: Amacom, 1982), foreword, p. xiv.

CHAPTER FOUR

The Public Policy Process and Corporate Viability

The public policy process is the mechanism in a free society by which the public's aspirations and dissatisfactions work their way up through public issue debates into law and regulation, if they are not voluntarily resolved in the private sector.

Its relevance to the business community has been long recognized by a handful of scholars for many decades, although only practically acknowledged by business practitioners during the last 15 to 20 years. For example, economist John M. Clark wrote before World War II, "The community of free exchange cannot maintain itself except in the enveloping medium of a broader community life, which furnishes the conditions on which free exchange depends and stands ready to do the innumerable things it leaves undone and to care for interests which it neglects."[1]

It is society's ability to control business through the public policy process that prompted Clark's observation that "private business is no longer private, as this phrase was used 100 years ago." Generations of strong-willed, but frustrated business executives attest to the truth of Clark's insight. Scholars in this half of the 20th century (especially George Cabot Lodge) have concluded that what the public policy process has effected is a companion "right" to the time-honored "right of private property," which historically has been the main responsibility of code law to pro-

---

[1]John W. Clark, *Social Control of Business* (New York: McGraw-Hill, 1939), p. xii.

tect and conserve. That new right, which began to emerge in the depression-ridden years of the 1930s, was the "right of membership." Rights of membership in U.S. society began to erode property rights when federal and then state governments, through income tax laws, began to redistribute income from one class to less fortunate income classes.

These efforts at first were desperate measures to keep families and individuals alive, barely above the level of subsistence— and were generally supported by both the haves and the have nots. By the end of the 1930s and on into the post-World War II period, social experimenters realized that legislatures could be used not only to redistribute income through tax laws, but also to achieve other social goals—minimum wages, worker safety, minority rights, and cultural support, for example. That is, the public policy process gave any organized group, not merely the two established political parties, the power to use laws as the major tool for social change. And the business community was always viewed as an essential element in bringing about desired social change. That is, planners outside the business community advanced ambitious programs for more social equity to be either paid for or effected by the business community through coercive legislation, for the planners had little faith in voluntary cooperation from business.

Business managers, as a class, watched these changes occur and understood them in their role as citizens, but viewed them with little understanding and tried to reject them in their role as managers. Today, many managers, especially those with experience in using an issues management process for their companies, now understand the central meaning of the public policy process.

That meaning is simple: All major issues any corporation faces in its sociopolitical and economic environments are *cost-shifting* issues, as the Nobel-winning economist George J. Stigler has demonstrated in his many essays. One group in society seeks to shift the cost of a benefit it wants to another group or the business world or the government. Because these groups of organized citizens usually do not have marketplace power (wealth or economic influence), they convert an economic issue into a sociopolitical issue by appealing to equity—to fairness. Thus, corporate issues in the public policy process can always be viewed as a clash between *efficiency* (the goal of all business enterprises) and *equity* (the goal of all citizen-based groups and, presumably, their elected representatives, the government).

There is nothing inherently wrong or evil about this process, if you believe in both the free enterprise system and our democratic process, for both imply: (1) citizens deserve freedom because they are capable of looking after their own interests, and (2) if they cannot look after those interests as individuals, they can appeal to the public forums where open debate will develop sufficient information for society to protect those interests. Of course, individual interests must give way to larger public interests when those are determined, thereby providing the necessary check on rampant individualism, which unchecked would destroy any society. However, those actors in our society who do not fully comprehend the emergence of the new rights and the expanded use of the public policy process are at a terrible disadvantage as they face the future.

One of the best ways to understand the public policy process as it relates to business and the issues management tool is to examine the Yankelovich, Skelly, and White description, which I have reduced to a simplified graphic model (see Figure 4–1).

The base of the pyramid indicates public dissatisfaction with the present. The public expresses a desire for the realization of some long-held or newly formulated aspiration—such as better education, homeownership, job security, or safety. Such dissatisfaction can take the form of concern over a real or imagined wrong or the belief that a right is being ignored. Not much happens at this level until the dissatisfaction gets a name, a label.

Once it gets a name—welfare rights, consumer rights, fair housing, redlining, nuclear ban, women's rights—the media can pick it up and start to talk about it. The media don't create these issues, although most senior officers mistakenly believe they do, but they do play a key role in issue development, in its life cycle. (Every time the print or electronic news media attempt to create an issue, they always fail unless their depiction in fact describes underlying reality, for the fierce public debate that ensues from parties at interest blows unfounded "issues" off the top of the news in short time.)

After the news media take the issue to a broader audience, nothing really happens until a pressure group takes note of the issue and decides to add it to its agenda. After the activist group—

FIGURE 4-1   Public Policy Process Model (social control of business)

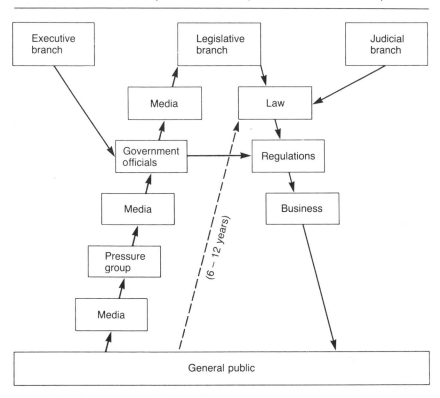

public interest group, chambers of commerce, trade association, religious institution, political party—takes up the issue and begins to create pressure, the group's ultimate effectiveness is determined by how well it can mobilize social and political forces beyond its own membership. The media, of course, are critical at this point. That is why groups hold public demonstrations and meetings and make headline-grabbing statements. Thus, the group becomes the issue champion and, in effect, co-opts it.

When an industry or an individual corporation is involved, activists usually approach the company and demand a "bargaining" or "negotiating" meeting, complete with notice to the media. If the company or industry does not respond satisfactorily, the activist group goes to the appropriate regulatory agency, again with notice to the media. By this stage, the actions have churned up enough public attention that regulators begin paying attention, either because of their regulatory responsibility or because, as in the case of the Federal Trade Commission, they would like more regulatory power over the industry or issue involved.

Regulators receive complaints and studies from citizen groups, make their own studies, and hold their own public hearings. All these activities have the potential for increasing news value and attention.

Finally, the elected legislative officials stand at the apex of the public policy process, brokering conflicting demands, bending to their key publics—if they think there is sufficient public consensus to justify a legislative solution to the process. Thus, a new law and regulations promulgated under it come down on the business community like a restrictive cap.

It should be noted that an issue does not have to travel the whole route from the general public to legislative consideration, but can emerge and start to move at any point on the process model—at the pressure group level, the government officials level, or at the legislative level. Also, every issue is not resolved by the enactment of a law. Many are not capable of legislative solutions. In some of those cases, extrajudicial solutions are frequently sought through direct pressure by citizens groups, peer pressure, and voluntary agreements between conflicting groups or voluntary codes of conduct within an industry, profession, or civic association.

This process model accounts for most of the good and bad changes that have happened in the business world during the past five decades. Unfortunately, the business world has had a sorry history in this process. According to former Securities and Exchange Commission Chairman Harold Williams, the business community ignores the developing forces until it is too late. It leaps in at the regulatory or legislative enactment stage, when it can do little more than hope to moderate the dire consequences of the legislation. At this stage, regulators and legislators view the business community as the cause of the problem; they don't look to business for solutions. That is why business is famous for killing legislation. It has no respectable record of proposing and supporting enactment of broadly creative legislation. This lagging response prevailed until the issues management process emerged.

Informed managers began to realize that they must intervene

in the process well before the regulatory/legislative confrontation stage when possible. They then have the hope of helping guide the process with the other participants. However, this hope is possible only if they work at early recognition of issues on the local and national levels as they emerge and then resolve to participate in the developing process.

Although business has had a minor role, citizen and special interest participation in the public policy process has expanded dramatically as public interest groups, consumer groups, environmental groups, neighborhood organizations, and thousands of single-issue groups awoke to its possibilities. And during this time, institutions have consistently misread what was happening. For example, California's Proposition 13 movement was widely viewed as a one-time "tax revolt." Actually, because of the dilatory actions of the California legislature, citizens decided to bypass representative government and opt for participatory government—they took the legislative power back into their own hands on this one issue. This has happened in all the states that give the power of referenda and initiative to its residents.

Although the forces bringing about the democratic or social control of business seem to have sprung up recently, the process has been underway in the United States for more than a century. Commencing with the effective control of railroads and utilities at the turn of this century, the social control of business has been developing at an accelerating pace.

As one observer of the public policy process noted years ago, "It may be guided and directed, its movement made more informed and enlightened, but it cannot be stopped, and no one group can dictate its course."

Research specialists have found that issues emerging at the public level of the model never reach final enactment into law at the federal level in less than six years, although they can move in one to two years at the state and local level under extreme circumstances. Most federal solutions take 12 or more years to legislative resolution. For example, William L. Renfro, president of the Policy Analysis Co., Inc., has tracked the 13-year path of the Employee Retirement Income Security Act of 1974 to illustrate the time lag involved. It began in 1962 under President Kennedy when he appointed a commission to study the issues. The commission issued its report in 1965, bills were debated in

Congress through 1973. In 1974 the conference bill passed both houses and President Ford signed the Security Act, ERISA (P.L. 93–406), into law that year.

Thus, business institutions have no excuse for being surprised when an issue emerges at the national level, for it is clear that they would have had plenty of time to develop their own plans and suggested solutions if they were tracking issues as they emerge. The process model in Figure 4–2 shows some of the ways issues can be scanned for, identified, and tracked.

Many public issues affecting business can be resolved well below the legislative stage if the company has been tracking and analyzing them early in their development stage and participating with the parties at interest in the voluntary creation of solutions. One of the goals of issues management is to reduce

FIGURE 4–2   Public Policy Process Model

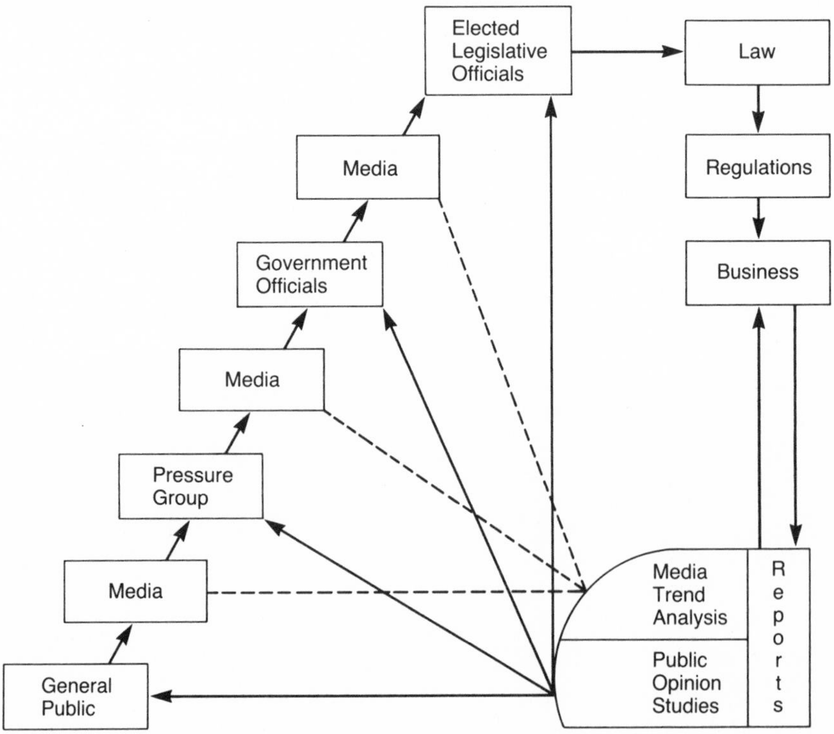

legislative solutions, except when that is the only option open or is necessary because of the range of an issue.

It is clear today that every corporation or business enterprise has to be willing to participate in the public policy process at certain stages of its development, either alone if necessary or in a "convoy" organized by its trade association. This is not only necessary for its survival at times; it is also one of the few paths open to create a favorable environment for viable growth and success. In fact, it is essential to managing the corporation's new bottom line.

CHAPTER FIVE _____

Issues Management: A Systems Management Process

Early on, practitioners recognized that issues management is a process. It never produces one "product" in the sense that strategic planning does—"the business plan" that can be referred to any time during the year.

Issues management is a process designed to focus on high-priority problems and trends affecting key stakeholder groups for the purpose of developing policy and plans to guide day-to-day decision making in the successful operation of a corporation. As noted above, it is not a product in the sense of voluminous reports, operating manuals, and so on, which the minions of an organization can mindlessly follow. Nor is it a silver bullet, a magic formula to remove all problems. It is a management systems process designed to efficiently utilize the human problem-solving resources of the institution. And it can be fitted to any company or organization according to its needs and available resources.

The *function* of issues management, according to W. Howard Chase, is "to manage both profit and policy by disciplined process—not by visceral impulse." Its objective, he points out, is "to participate in formation of public policy that affects an institution, instead of being the end of the crack-the-whip line dominated by external, and usually adversarial, forces."[1] (Chase, broadly acknowledged as the "father" of issues management, has

_____
[1] W. H. Chase, *Issue Management: Origins of the Future* (Stamford, Conn.: Issue Action Publications, 1984), unnumbered page preceding table of contents.

written an excellent book, *Issue Management: Origins of the Future,* which traces the events and thinking behind the development of the issues management process.)

Chase's points are well taken. Business historically has taken a limited view of its place in the national environment. Attempting to restrict its concern to the economic sphere, it believed it had a small or no legitimate role to play in the broad sociopolitical spheres, except when its survival was at stake. Critics of business have reinforced that perception.

This attitude resulted in an unprecedented battering of business from the 1960s to the present. Unanticipated demands welling up from the sociopolitical side of the environment during the past several decades resulted in a drastic drop in the public's respect for business—from 70 percent approval in 1968 to a low of about 15 percent by 1978, although it has been slowly recovering toward the 20 percent range since. This resulted in a marked increase in the government's unwillingness to let business manage its operations free from regulation and restrictions. The result has been a steadily increasing financial and economic impact on private corporations, with greater percentages of senior management time and corporate budgets being devoted to public issue debate and legislation. For example, a Conference Board study revealed that by 1976, 96 percent of 181 CEOs polled spent from 25 to 50 percent more of their time on public issues, a startling increase over the amount of time they had spent on such matters only five years earlier.

The advent of President Reagan's administration temporarily put a halt to increased regulation, but the process will probably start again at the federal level when he leaves the White House. Even during his term, regulatory activity picked up at the state level, where issue champions shifted their attention when they found the Washington environment less friendly.

Issues management, as public policy foresight and planning for corporations, emerged in response to changed business environment in the closing decades of the 20th century.

ISSUES MANAGEMENT: THE PROCESS MODEL

A consensus description of issues management developed by 10 of us who are experienced practitioners can be summarized as follows: Issues management contributes to the strategic management process of a corporation when it is utilized by senior management. In its foresight function, it provides crucial intelligence on social, economic, political, and technological trends, events, and developments affecting the corporation's current success and future viability. In its planning function, it establishes an agenda for and a means of marshaling participation in the public policy process when high-impact issues reach that forum.

The issues management process model developed in 1977 by Chase and an associate, Barrie L. Jones, is the basic model all subsequent models have built on. The model is based on the assumption: "No company can simultaneously manage every issue. Therefore, companies need to develop procedures for identifying and sorting out the issues of primary concern to their current operations." Chase's model involves five steps:

1. Issue identification—primary identification of specific issue.
2. Issue analysis—results in judgment and priority setting.
3. Issue change strategy options—policy developed and supporting change strategy plan created.
4. Issue action programming—execution of plan by line and staff.
5. Evaluation of results—degree of success assessed; issue monitored to see if it is metamorphosing into a new issue.

PPG Industries, an early user of the process, saw issues management as:

1. Issue identification.
2. Impact assessment.
3. Position formulation.
4. Action-plan development and implementation.
5. Communications.

In 1978, Allstate developed the following seven-step system:

1. Staff identification of emerging issues (scanning).
2. Prioritization of issues, selection by chairman of Issues Management Committee of only the four to five highest-priority issues for current attention (staff continuing to monitor the remaining issues for changes).
3. Carefully selected issue task forces engage in extensive

research, stakeholder impact analysis, and development of policy options and related supporting program plans for each high-priority issue.

4. Policy selection with supporting program plan made by senior officer, Issues Management Committee.
5. Issue strategy program implemented by departments reporting to senior officers of the Issues Management Committee.
6. Communication to the appropriate stakeholders.
7. Evaluation of results by staff leader for Issues Management Committee to determine if adjustments in policy and programs are required.

The issues management system was designed to recognize that all public issues have a wave-like life cycle, sometimes lying dormant for months or years at certain stages only to spring up and sweep like a tide through the public forums. The concern of business was best expressed by former General Electric planner, Ian H. Wilson, in these terms: "The social concerns of yesterday become the political issues of today, the legislated requirements of tomorrow, and the litigated penalties of the day after." This cycle can be expressed by Figure 5–1.

The goal of issues management is to identify a significant issue early in its cycle, when corporate options are broad and the potential for multiple options are broadest. The four stages in the life cycle of an issue were identified and analyzed by a congressional private sector task force, whose 10 members (including this author) were drawn from the issues management and strategic planning staffs of their companies. (See Appendix: "Foresight in the Private Sector: How Can Government Use It?"; report of the Foresight Task Force to the Committee on Energy and Commerce, U.S. House of Representatives, January 1983.)

These developments of an issue occur during four stages:

* The Societal Expectations stage signals structural changes in society, giving rise to media recognition, and, if not resolved in the private sector, political recognition of the issue.
* Political Developments stage gives rise to the creation of ad hoc groups and formal organizations to advance an issue solution.

FIGURE 5-1   Life Cycle of a Strategic Issue

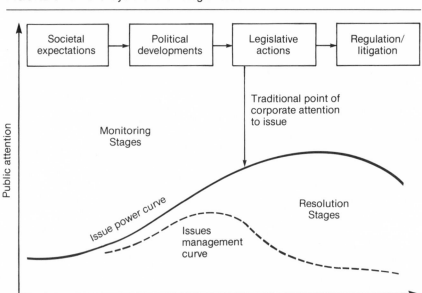

- The Legislative Actions stage signals a peak in public attention to the isue, when it is defined in operational or legal terms and solutions, and frequently results in the passage of laws and the promulgation of regulations.
- The Regulation/Litigation stage represents a plateau in public attention, when the law is tested in the courts, enforcement becomes routine, and penalties are applied to those who ignore or violate the spirit, letter, and/or intent of the law.

ISSUE ANALYSIS

The Conference Board, which has periodically surveyed corporate issues management practices, developed the following definition of an issue from its research: "An issue is a condition or pressure, either internal or external to an organization, that, if it continues, will have a significant effect on the functioning of the organization or its future interests."[2]

The board's studies reveal that industry specialists usually divide issues into three categories according to their stage of development:

- Current issues—those that are moving toward resolution and are usually in the legislative or regulatory process. These are current operational issues being handled by the appropriate functional departments under existing policy and strategy.
- Emerging issues—those whose definition and contending positions are evolving and legislation or regulation is likely in a moving time frame of one-and-a-half to three years in the future. These are the ones issues management staffs are concerned with.
- Strategic issues—those that are important in long-range planning, with probable impact being felt in from 4 to 20 years in the future. These are the ones that long-range business planners take into account in developing the corporate strategic plan.

The preliminary stage of issue analysis seeks to determine the answers to the following questions:

1. Is the issue primarily internal or external?
2. Is it a political or legislative/regulatory issue, or is it primarily economic or social?
3. What stage of development is it in? Is it an emerging, a strategic, or a current issue?
4. How long has it been around? Is it really new, or an old issue that has been repackaged and re-energized?
5. What will or could be the nature of its impact on the corporation? Will that be direct or indirect?
6. Can the corporation affect the issue's development and successful resolution? If not, can industry associations and coalitions be organized to affect it? If neither, it is merely an issue to be monitored and management kept informed, without resources being assigned to it. Of

---

[2]J. K. Brown, "This Business of Issues: Coping with the Company's Environments" (New York: The Conference Board, 1979), p. 1.

course, continual monitoring will alert management to any opportunities should the issue's nature change and conditions change, which would permit the corporation or its industry to favorably impact it.

7. Is the issue a bottom-line, profit-threatening one? Or is it an issue that will broadly affect the public domain, having equal impact on the company, its competitors, and the business community in general? Bottom-line issues not only affect profitability and shareholders, but other stakeholders as well. Hence, they are always examined early and carefully.

8. What is the regional and structural impact of the issue? Is it global, multinational, national, or local? Does it affect business in general, one or more industries, your company, a company component, or any of your primary stakeholders?

9. Who are the major *movers* of the issue and what positions have they already adopted, or are they likely to adopt?

After the issues management staff completes this preliminary analysis of emerging issues, each issue is given an initial priority analysis. Issues managers sometimes use 4, 6, 12 or 16 box matrices for this analysis. The basic four-box matrix is sufficient for the preliminary priority analysis. A simplified version of one developed by SRI International for threat assessment purposes has the virtue of quickly rank ordering each issue (see Figure 5–2). Only issues in quadrants I and II need senior management policy attention.

From the discussion thus far, it is clear that all issues management systems actually used by corporations and other institutions have two types of tasks: (1) the front-end scanning, research, analysis, and options recommending tasks primarily handled by experienced and professional staff managers; and (2) the decision-making and program-initiating tasks of senior management. The next chapters look at those tasks.

FIGURE 5–2   Threat Assessment

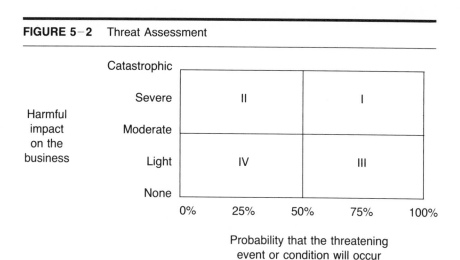

Probability that the threatening
event or condition will occur

CHAPTER SIX

How the Issues Management System Operates

All viable issues management systems involve the participation of many layers of management and specialists within the organization. The most successful have a high degree of top-down, bottom-up participation during different phases of issues research, analysis, and planning.

This is not only necessary to marshal and effectively use the essential knowledge and creative resources within the organization; it also generates a valuable by-product—team building, not only among senior managers, but among middle and junior management as well. Was there ever a manager below the most senior level who has never complained about "not being consulted" by senior management when major policy and planning decisions were made? The issues management process has a place for this input before policy is finalized. And management staff is grateful.

At the same time a rational issues management system generates these benefits from existing talent available within a company, it is also cost effective. It is cost effective because the staff assigned full time to issues management work need not be large. The full-time staff need be no larger than one director or manager, with no more than one to three assistants, or none if the director is at least a 10-year employee with considerable knowledge of the company and its industry. Most staff directors have extensive experience in their companies' public affairs or public relations operations, a large network of outside contacts, and knowledge of information sources. They also have an understanding of both senior management's vision of their companies and, equally important, their companies' unique corporate culture.

Personnel assigned to issues management research and analysis spend full time at the work, not engaging in current management of functional departments or operations. Others needed in the process can be temporarily included in certain work phases without forgoing their normal daily departmental assignments. This permits all preliminary staff work to be done before issues are brought before senior management for final discussions and decision making. Thus, senior management time is conserved, needed only in one- to two-hour periods a month on a scheduled basis. The system is not only cost effective in terms of professional staff size, it is also cost effective in terms of use of senior officer time, the most expensive in the corporation.

All publicly held corporations are literally drenched with information, every department awash in data, historical files, incoming communications, and more. The issues management staff's job is to develop its system to work through "nice-to-know" information to find the "need-to-know" information that can be summarized and packaged in a form upper management can digest and use in directing the company toward its goals. This can be done without developing exotic techniques or buying or creating "new" systems or magic issue finders. The first models developed by Chase and refined by practitioners, as discussed in the preceding chapter, need merely be adapted to the needs of the company. Special refinements will suggest themselves to the staff as circumstances and needs of their company demand. Spending months researching systems and creating the unique issues management system for one company merely delays getting at the task at hand—identifying and dealing with the company's most significant public issues.

ISSUE IDENTIFICATION

The first job of the issues management staff is to identify on an ongoing basis the emerging issues relevant to the company's universe. This is the *scanning* phase (see Figure 6–1). It has been described by practitioners as the radar-sweep phase. Staff is looking for the first blip of an incoming issue missile. The scan is

FIGURE 6-1 Major Environments of Business

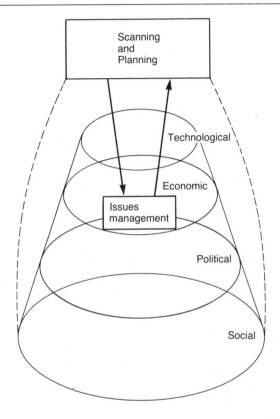

done externally by reading current periodicals, books, symposia reports, and newsletters, and by attending both industry and other meetings and conferences where new developments and trends are discussed by speakers and panels.

Scanning is also done internally by personal discussions with the most knowledgeable management and professional staff within the company. Home office and field managers and supervisors are surveyed annually or semiannually for their nominations of the five most important issues they think their company faces. However, the best place to start and then to check annually are the five-year strategic plans of the company's business units. Each usually contains its own environmental and competitive analysis, where professional managers identify the important issues facing their profit centers. Although analysis of these

plans results in the collection of hundreds of issues, many dupli-
cative, they can all be categorized into between 5 and 10 issue
"clusters." This lets staff begin to see the overall environmental
patterns forming about their company. Internal scanning collects
emerged issues that already have been recognized by the company's management.

The staff's primary job, however, is to recognize emerging
issues at the earliest stage possible. The longest-running business trend and issue scanning system has been operated by the
American Council of Life Insurance. Up to 200 member-company
employees scan publications for its Trend Analysis Program.
Although ACLI's TAP program scans more than 150 publications
on a regular basis, most company systems scan between 20 and 50
mass media, scientific, and trade publications. Companies that
use only one or two staff members in an issues management
system scan 10 to 15 publications and buy issue-scanning reports
from private consulting and research organizations that provide
this service.

The two leading suppliers of issue identification and trend
tracking services based on media and other analysis are: HRN,
1926 Arch Street, Philadelphia, PA 19103, which publishes two
services, *Stakeholder Issues & Strategies* and *IssueTrack*; and the
firm of Weiner, Edrich, Brown, Inc., 200 East 33rd Street, New
York, NY 10016. Other issue and trend services are supplied by
John Naisbitt's organization, SRI International, The Futures
Group (Glastonbury, Conn.), William Renfro's Policy Analysis
Co., Inc. (Washington, D.C.), and various regional services.

The World Future Society publishes two trend and forecasting reporting services, *Future Survey* and *Futures Research
Quarterly*, in addition to its *Futurist* magazine. It is located at
4916 St. Elmo Avenue, Bethesda, MD 20814.

Sociopolitical issue reports affecting corporations, based on
public surveys and research, are available from the following: the
newly formed Yankelovich Group (issue research service headed
by Madelyn Hochstein and the former Corporate Priorities staff
of YSW), Lou Harris, ORC, The Cambridge Reports, Roper, and
other social research and polling organizations.

The leading newsletter reporting on issues management developments is *Corporate Public Issues*, which was founded by W.
Howard Chase and is published at 105 Old Long Ridge Road,

Stamford, CT 06903. The most widely used newsletter based on media content analysis and percentage of coverage given public issues affecting corporations is the *Issues Management Letter*, published at 300 North Washington Street, Suite 401, Alexandria, VA 22314.

Another valuable source for trend forecasting and issue identification is the United Way of America, United Way Plaza, Alexandria VA 22314 2088. It publishes periodically an updated environmental scan report, *What Lies Ahead—A New Look*, a decade-long look into the future. This report and its various manuals on environmental analysis, issue identification techniques, and trend forecasting are the product of issues managers, strategic planners, and public relations/public affairs executives from more than 40 companies who sit on its Environmental Scanning Committee and its Strategic Process Committee. United Way Vice President Dr. George Wilkenson directs the work of these committees and the internal planning staff. These committees, under the leadership of veteran issues managers Lynne Hall of Hall and Associates and William C. Ashley of United Airlines, have become the major network center for corporate, governmental, and consulting professionals in the foresight and planning field. The high quality of United Way's publications reflects both the expert input of its committees and the professionalism of the United Way staff.

It should be noted, however, that these outside reports and services are used primarily to support the work of the corporate issues management staff. They do not replace the important internal staff issue scanning.

Staff must scan on a regular basis both the company-specific publications (trade and scientific journals) and the broader mass media and specialized publications reflecting social, political, and economic changes occurring in contemporary society. Since new issues and novel solutions for them most frequently appear first in professional, academic, and counterculture publications and books, staff must devise a system to cover these developments.

In addition to the World Future Society's *Future Survey*, which contains digests of these books and reports, the book review sections of newspapers and magazines must be scanned. The reason is simple. Historical research has revealed that one or two persons in academe, government service, or professional consulting work are usually the first to see and identify massive trends or social changes occurring. Their lonely articles, reports, and fulminations frequently are the first sign that an issue has been born. Since these invariably begin in print form, despite the electronic news media's enormous mass audience, issues managers must turn first to print scanning. Public events that are the grist for electronic journalists' mill occur later, after the issue begins to move.

Veteran corporate issues managers usually personally scan the following publications:

Newspapers:

> *Christian Science Monitor*
> *New York Times* (especially Sunday edition)
> *Washington Post* (especially weekly edition)
> *The Wall Street Journal*
> *U.S.A. Today*
> Metropolitan papers of company's headquarter city

Periodicals:

> *American Demographics*
> *Business Week*
> *CoEvolution Quarterly*
> *The Economist*
> *Forbes*
> *Fortune*
> *Mother Jones*
> *Newsweek*
> *New York Review of Books*
> *Public Opinion*
> *Rolling Stone*
> *Science*
> *Time*
> *U.S. News & World Report*
> *Vital Speeches of the Day*
> *Working Women*
> *World Press Review* (especially for the political cartoons, which frequently are the first explicit depiction of a new sociopolitical or economic issue)

Additional publications identified and recommended by other issues managers are added when merited, but the above are the basic publications necessary for scanning the general environment of any company. In addition, since all activist organizations publish their own newsletters and reports, these as well as underground publications should be regularly checked if possible. Since most issues managers don't have access to all of these publications, many subscribe to HRN's *IssueTrack* newsletter, which does subscribe to most of these types of publications and regularly scans them for the service.

The scanning task has phases of informal, general information gathering, and formal, abstract writing. The informal phase adds general understanding to the staff scanner's knowledge base. The formal phase is used when significant issues or trends are identified. The criteria below, adapted from those developed by the ACLI TAP system, are useful as guidelines for selecting articles to write abstracts on:

1. Does the article represent new events, ideas, trends, or issues that seem to foreshadow change?
2. Does the article contradict convential wisdom, your company or industry assumptions, or your own beliefs about what seems to be happening?
3. Is the article from a surprising source in terms of the author or the publication?
4. Does the article throw new light on research already done?
5. Does the article contain implications of significant magnitude that could have explicit or implicit bearing on the long-range concerns of your company and its stakeholders?

Benchmarks used by veteran scanners in deciding whether an abstract of the article is in order include:

Context: Has an issue jumped from one industry to another?
Has a public leader adopted a new issue?
Have arguments from one field been applied to a new one?

> Have new phrases or buzzwords emerged with the new issue or an old issue, reflecting a change in strategy?

Organization: Has a previously strong organization begun to lose power, members, and so on?
Has a new civic, political, social, or professional group been formed?
Has new leadership emerged for old or new groups?

Abstracts produced from article scanning are usually held to one page in length. They should contain source data: title, author, publication, date. The body of the abstract is devoted to a summary of the article, concluding with a brief paragraph on the implications that can be drawn from it. These abstracts generally have a code word assigned to them, naming the issue, issue cluster, or trend they relate to. Most issues managers keep these in drop files, although companies with sophisticated computer databases developed for both issues management and strategic planning environmental analysis purposes move them into a special corporate database. However, since most of these abstracts have a short shelf life and can be easily located in the future through commercially available literature search computer systems (company librarians are expert at these searches), I doubt the value of creating extensive computer databases for this purpose. It is too costly and eats up too much staff time inside the company. However, if such databases have real value, a trade association can be easily persuaded to develop them for a whole industry, with the cost shared by the member companies.

After staff has made its emerging-issue identification survey, issue briefs need to be written for each major issue or issue cluster. These briefs are usually one page in length, headed with the name of the issue, a one- or two-sentence definition or description of it, and a short summary of its potential positive or negative impact on the company's future if it is left to develop alone under the forces and actors driving it. This summary indicates the staff's estimates of the issue's stages of future development, threat to the company's viability, and of the company's or industry's ability to effect its resolution.

ISSUE PRIORITIZATION

These briefs of major issues (usually ranging from 5 to 10 in number) are submitted to the company's issues steering committee, composed of one or more senior officers. The steering committee does the final prioritization of the issues submitted and selects four or five of them for in-depth analysis and policy development. The company as a unit can focus on only about four or five issues at the most in any one year. Experience has shown that that is about the limit of the effective span of attention. Of course, other issues can be simultaneously handled by individual departments, but multidepartmental issues have to be dealt with by the top senior management team. Staff continues to monitor the remaining issues in the normal course of their work.

RESEARCH AND POLICY OPTION DEVELOPMENT

The high-priority issues selected for further work can be handled in one of two ways.

In smaller companies, the issues management staff itself does the additional research, makes the stakeholder impact analysis, and develops the menu of policy options and operational programs for each of them.

In larger companies with more sophisticated managerial and professional staff resources, the steering committee sets up issue task forces to study and develop recommended policy and action plans. The committee, usually with issues management staff recommendations, carefully determines the kind of members each task force requires. Then, the functional departments that either will be impacted by the issue or have expertise in understanding the issue are identified. Next, if the company's corporate culture and/or the senior status of the steering committee officers permit the action, the committee itself picks both the task force leader and the individuals by name from the functional departments, based on their experience, intelligence, and expertise. Where tradition and corporate culture does not permit this, task force member selection is deferred to the officers in charge of each affected department. In any case, the issues management staff serves as both a resource staff and ex-officio advisors to each task force.

I recommend that, when possible, the first method of selection of individuals be by the steering committee, because too many department officers have hidden personal and political agendas relating to their own careers that determine their selection of personnel for task force duty. These agendas have little relevance to issues management work and can weaken the quality of the task force's output, especially when less qualified or recalcitrant persons are selected to serve.

The importance of having the best talent on each issue task force cannot be overstated. For task force membership, the company is not restricted to the officer or upper middle management levels. It can dig deep into its middle and junior management ranks, if the people sought are distinctly qualified. This procedure not only gets the benefit of top-down, bottom-up thinking, it also has the benefit of training more junior managers for future responsibilities.

Dedicated and professional managers have two roles on every task force. First, they represent their department's knowledge and interests on the task force; second, they represent the entire company's interest in arriving at the final task force recommendations. Thus, they have the job of presenting their department's and department officer's ideas and recommendations in the task force's early deliberations. However, in reaching the task force's final recommendations, they have the job of representing the entire company's overall best interest.

In this role, they must sometimes come down in favor of a policy or program option their own department or department officer opposes. When this occurs, however, they must insist that their department's opposition to the task force's recommendation be presented fairly in the final report. Obviously, this second role of representing the entire company's interest requires not only intellectual integrity, but personal courage as well, since the member could find himself or herself in an unfavorable position with departmental peers. The senior status of the steering committee officers and the guidelines they set down for task force members' duties usually protect all task force participants from any unfavorable backlash. In fact, when this occasionally occurs, the department head and the member's peers point with pride to their objectivity, affirming their department members' professionalism and loyalty to the overall interests of the company.

ISSUE POLICY AND STRATEGY SELECTION

Issue task force's final report to the senior management group that must make the final decisions usually contains:

- A statement of the issue.
- Background and detailed analysis based on research.
- A set of forecasts or scenarios of relevance to the company's future, based on probability estimates.
- Analysis of any current company policy relating to the issue.
- Modified current policy or new policy options open to the company, with appropriate operational programs planned to effect the goals of each policy.
- Finally, the task force's recommended policy and supporting program.

The last portion of the report is very important, for without its recommendation as to the best policy to adopt, the task force has not completed staff work. This requirement is not only important to assure that the task force works to its best level of expertise, but it gives senior management reliable evidence of the quality of talent the company has at its second and third levels of managers for future needs. Finally, the task force's recommendations as to policy are important because its members, of all managers within the company, have made the most serious and in-depth study of the issue. Their informed judgment is of great value to senior management in preparing to make the final decisions.

In this author's experience, issue task force's work and recommendations usually are adopted, with appropriate modifications based on the senior officers' broader knowledge of the company's other goals, future changes, and other factors.

PROGRAM EXECUTION

Once policy has been selected, the issue strategy program is implemented through the appropriate departments involved—such as government relations, public relations, marketing, and personnel—according to the timetable developed for the program. This is usually effected through the senior officers involved in making the final policy decision.

The policy and program are communicated to the appropriate stakeholders (customers, employees, shareholders, or general public as their interests determine). This may be done through company publications, advocacy ads, shareholder letters or reports, or customer billing inserts.

Finally, the issues management staff leader has the duty of preparing periodic reports for the issues steering committee on the progress of the issue strategy program and the need, if any, for additional support or resources. In collecting information for progress reports, the issues management staff leader must be careful neither to interfere with functional departments' work in carrying out the issue strategy program nor be perceived as a "power broker" dealing with senior management. He or she is a facilitator with responsibility to help those responsible for carrying out the programs in support of corporate policy.

At this point, attention should be given to "the economics of information." The phrase was created by the Nobel prize-winning economist, George Stigler. His studies in this field indicate that all information costs the seeker and user money and time. He concluded that individuals and organizations will spend up to the amount of money acquiring information that the information's value represents to them in terms of cost savings and so on. Therefore, in allocating budget resources to the issues management staff, a company should not be overly stringent in budgeting for acquisition of relevant issue and trend information. This means that funds should be available not only for the purchase of periodicals, books, and research reporting services, but also for membership in appropriate professional and special-interest organizations, conference attendance fees, and staff travel. A company's issues management system is only as good as the relevance and reliability of its information base.

CHAPTER SEVEN

How to Fit the Process into Your Corporation

Being a process, issues management is not a rigid "system" that can operate only one way, with one type of organizational structure, staff, and procedures. Being a management process, it is flexible. It can be introduced into a subunit of a functional department for the guidance of the manager of that unit, or it can be introduced as a support system for the CEO and the other senior officers.

The important thing to know is that the most senior manager who wants the benefits of the system, whether that be the CEO or a department officer, determines its qualities, the issue range, the staff to be selected, and the use of its work. For example, if the government relations officer (usually called the public affairs officer, because of the public relations functions involved today) wants it, the issues management system will focus heavily on legislative/regulatory issues, such as proposed legislative and regulatory changes, in the near term. The range is short, 6 to 18 months in the future—this or the next legislative session. If the CEO introduces the process inside the company, it takes a much broader range of issues (social, political, economic, and technological), with a longer time frame (at least up to three years), and a more broadly skilled staff.

This means that the most senior officer or manager who wants and institutes the issues management system in the company determines (1) what issues management *is* in that company,

(2) the nature of the issues to be selected, (3) who will be selected for the issues management staff, and (4) whether the process will deal with companywide or only departmentwide policy.

This explains why no two issues management systems currently operating in major U.S corporations are exactly alike. That is evidence of the process' flexibility and adaptability. It also explains past failures and disappointments a few companies have had with their issues management systems.

Just as corporate planning, or strategic long-range planning, works well only in those companies that install it at the top level of the company first and then involve the relevant functional departments, so too issues management works best when introduced at the senior management level, involving in some manner all significant functional departments.

Thus, an issues management system can be a board of directors' committee function, a headquarters companywide function, a departmental function, or a departmental subunit function (usually bootlegged into the company by a bright unit manager who was unable to get the department officer to adopt the system for the whole department).

BOARD COMMITTEE PLUS INTERNAL COMMITTEE

One of the first companies to create a board of directors issues management system was the Bank of America. It created a seven-member Public Policy Committee, with six outside directors and one senior bank officer. The committee's function was to oversee the bank's public policy activities and to review the work of the company's Social Policy Committee.

The Social Policy Committee was made up of senior bank officers, who represented most of the operating functions public policy affected, including line functions.

A full-time five-member staff under the late James F. Langton, senior vice president—public relations, worked with issues task forces and coordinated with the internal Social Policy Committee. Members of the issues task forces could be drawn from up to 180 bank officials. Under this system, the staff drew up annually a list of all issues; staff and the Social Policy Committee then ranked them, focusing on the high-priority issues. Task forces were created for each major issue. The issue was researched, defined, and policy changes, if needed, were recommended. Each task force submitted an interim report to the Social Policy Committee within four months and its final report in six months. After several years of operation, Langton estimated that 75 percent of the task forces' recommendations were accepted, 10 percent were modified, and 15 percent were rejected by the Social Policy Committee. Activities of the internal Social Policy Committee were periodically reported to the Board Public Policy Committee, which occasionally recommended issues for the internal committee's attention.

Sears, Roebuck and Co. established a board committee at approximately the same time, but without an internal senior officer committee. An issues management research staff in the headquarters Public Affairs Department performs the issue identification tasks and develops impact forecasts and policy position by consulting with appropriate senior officers. The staff director, John Snow, then submits a report to the board through the CEO. After the board has reviewed and discussed the staff work, the company analysis, forecasts, and policy are communicated to both headquarters departments and operating groups. Other major corporations have similar board committees with oversight responsibility, with internal staffs doing the issue workup.

SENIOR MANAGEMENT COMMITTEE

Board of directors' public policy committees emerged in the 1970s primarily at the instigation of outside directors who became concerned over the increasing public criticism of corporations' sense (or perceived lack thereof) of social responsibility. In other companies, as noted in Chapter One, CEOs and other senior officers perceived the need to develop an internal issues management planning system.

One of the first to develop a structured internal system, which placed responsibility for issues management at the senior officer level, was the Allstate Insurance Companies (see Figure 7-1). Although Allstate is a wholly owned subsidiary of Sears, it has been permitted a remarkable degree of independence of operation by the parent company since its incorporation in 1931. This is because insurance is a highly regulated industry, requiring professional, full-time managers experienced in the business. Up to

FIGURE 7–1   Allstate Issues Management Process

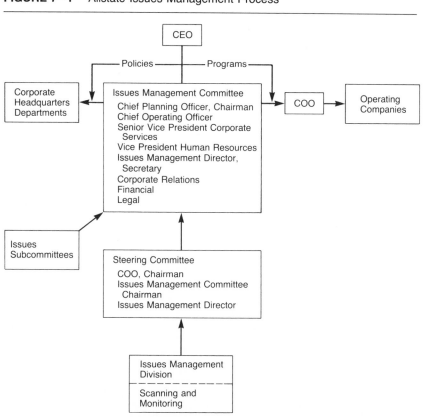

the present, all CEOs of Sears have come up through the parent's retail merchandising business. The parent intervenes primarily through Allstate's CEO, who is held responsible for the insurance group's overall results.

The Issues Management Committee is a matrix committee with its own broad-based policy charter. It is composed of the chief operating officer and the other senior officers who are responsible for all major corporate functions.

The committee reports to the CEO, but the CEO is not a member of the committee—for two reasons. First, that avoids adding additional work and time burdens unnecessarily on the CEO and provides a major decision-making support system for him. Secondly, it was recognized that his presence would inhibit free and open debate of all aspects of issues, proposed policies, and proposed programs by the other senior officers reporting to him. In short, serious disagreements as to proposed policy and programs are openly and fairly aired in the privacy of the committee meeting room so that the senior management team fully understands the implications of proposed policy. The policy is expanded and adjusted to anticipate any shortcomings identified. Only then is a consensus report passed up to the CEO.

Protocol deems that no senior officer can afterwards go on his own to the CEO and try to undo the committee decision; that person has to go back to the full committee and ask for a reconsideration of the position taken, giving reasons and expressing a willingness to accept the committee decision as to whether the matter will be reopened. This not only speeds up implementation of policy programs; it also avoids the malady many companies suffer from: the endless rechewing of old issues and alternative policies until action options have passed.

The committee makes the policy, supporting program, and budgeting decisions, deferring action only on those issues of a nature requiring CEO approval prior to implementation. (The COO is the committee member who decides when that approach is required.) The committee meets at least 10 times a year, usually in one-hour sessions, longer if special meetings are required. It deals annually with four to five high-priority issues expected to reach their resolution during the next 12 to 36 months. These issues are selected by the Steering Committee, which is chaired by the COO. (Richard J. Haayen, Allstate's Chairman and CEO since 1986, served as chairman of the Steering Committee from its inception in 1978 until becoming CEO in 1986.)

Issue subcommittees and task forces are chosen from the home office departments that have the necessary expertise and stake in the matter. Each subcommittee member represents both his or her department and the corporation; that is, the member is not restricted to considering or recommending policy and programs related only to the departmental function represented. The subcommittee can consider any policy alternatives it sees fit for recommendation to the full committee, even if the policy is a complete break with corporate tradition. There are no restrictions. Membership for these issue subcommittees is drawn from the officer ranks and from deep in the middle management staff.

The issue management director's job is to serve as secretary to the Issues Management Committee and the Steering Committee. He is also staff to both committees. His responsibilities include identifying emerging issues and monitoring identified ones. He presents to the Steering Committee summaries of major emerging issues for the committee's prioritization and scheduling to move before the full committee. He is also responsible for coordinating the issue subcommittees and their reporting schedules, as well as securing the necessary informational and other resources they need.

Allstate's Issues Management Division was located in the Corporate Relations (PR) Department for its first four years of existence, then moved to a newly formed Corporate Planning Department, which includes such functions as strategic planning and marketing planning.

Many other companies have developed similar senior management issue committees over the years. Monsanto took a path similar to Allstate's in 1982. John Hancock Insurance Co. used its Executive Committee as its senior officer issues committee, with the special issues management staff located in its public relations department. Other companies, such as Dow Chemical, ARCO, and Shell, have developed their own special systems, each involving senior management review at some stage. In every case, these companies have been able not only to set policy, but to implement it on a companywide basis.

The most noteworthy example of a senior management system developed by a trade association is the American Council of Life Insurance's model (see Figure 7–2).

The model begins with ACLI's long-running Trend Analysis Program (TAP), which involves a three-step scanning, analysis, and prioritization process. Volunteers (monitors) from member insurance companies read one of the more than 100 publications scanned. They prepare abstracts with their comments, which are topically coded and entered into ACLI's computer database.

These abstracts are reviewed by the Abstract Analysis Committee composed of member company and council staff specialists. The committee submits its issue and trend reports to the Steering Committee, which is composed of a small number of corporate and council officers. The Steering Committee decides

---

FIGURE 7-2 American Council of Life Insurance Trends Analysis Program (TAP)

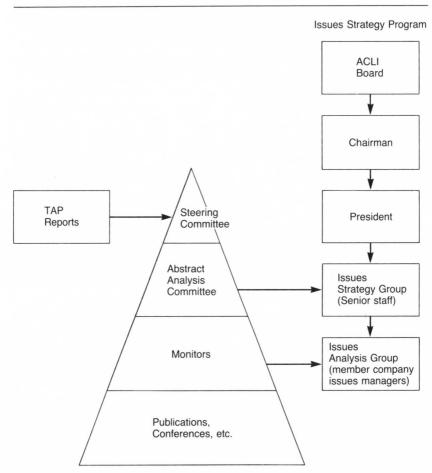

Issues Strategy Program

how the information will be used and reviews TAP reports that are distributed to member companies prior to publication.

The TAP process also feeds information to ACLI's Issues Strategy Program. This information and other issue data are analyzed by an Issues Analysis Group, composed of 10 issues managers from member companies and 4 council staff specialists. The group submits its issue list and recommendations to the Issues Strategy Group, composed of senior staff officers of the council. This group in turn recommends policy and action programs to the council's full-time president, who in turn submits recommendations to the council's board of directors, composed of member-company officers. This method not only utilizes the professional resources of the member companies and the council itself, it slowly builds an issue consensus as it reaches its final stage by the time recommendations are submitted to the board for final determination.

Many corporations have experimented with their own internal trend analysis committees, using experts on a voluntary basis from various functional departments. In my experience, after a year or so these internal corporate committees run out of new issues and trends and begin to focus on operational management problems. They can generate into sophisticated "bitch" sessions. This leaves the issues management director two choices: to become an informal back channel for reporting current operating problems and staff dissatisfactions to senior management behind the backs of the department officers affected, or to disband the committee. I disbanded my committee, deciding back-channel reporting on current morale and operating problems was neither forecasting nor cost-effective work for my division.

Another company that tried the trend analysis committee approach used bright middle managers. They became stimulated with the issues they identified, critical of their company's method of handling them, and angry over their department's lack of appreciation of their "unique" foresight talents. All of the younger ones sought and got jobs with other companies, and the trend committee collapsed from lack of members. The point being, when this type of committee is used in a corporation's issues management system, a good procedural plan must be developed for it, and the company culture must be flexible enough to openly acknowledge the value of the participating employees' contributions.

CHAPTER EIGHT

Issues Management Forecasting Techniques

Forecasting techniques are essential tools in any issues management system, whether applied formally or informally. The centrality of these tools is apparent when the broadest definition of issues management is considered: public policy foresight and planning.

To the casual observer major trends and issues seem to be the product of some giant random generator embedded in our society, completely incapable of anticipation or prediction. However, after years of research and analysis, experienced observers have concluded that they are subject to anticipation and forecasting.

The difference between these two types of observers can be accounted for by an observation Aristotle made more than 2,000 years ago. He wrote, "Men do not think they know a thing till they have grasped the 'why' of it." Both the hard and soft sciences, the physical and social sciences, have attacked the why of things since their beginnings. The result has been the formulation of laws and theories that purport to be capable of explaining a subject and predicting its behavior. As to the latter, H. G. Wells, in arguing for a "science of the future" 85 years ago, pointed out that "Until scientific theory yields confident forecasts, you know it is unsound and tentative."[1]

---

[1]H. G. Wells, "The Discovery of the Future," speech before the Royal Institution of England, 1902; reported in *Nature* 65, no.1684, p. 329.

Wells was talking about the physical sciences, not the social sciences, which are concerned with sociopolitical and economic forecasts. In issues management, we know we are not capable of absolute predictions, which implies an exactness as to timing of events, but of conditional predictions or forecasts, which deal with conjecture as to a range of alternative possibilities.

Although there are many elegant and elaborate definitions of forecasting, I prefer Bertrand de Jouvenel's simple formulation: "Forecasting consists of passing from knowledge about present conditions to estimates of future conditions."[2]

Jouvenel's taxonomy of types of forecasts, when adapted for issues management research and analysis purposes, is also insightful and reasonably exhaustive. The three types are:

- *Primary forecasts*, which are conditional predictions, given our knowledge of present conditions, as to what will happen over a span of time if there is no conscious intervention and present trends are allowed to play themselves out. Primary forecasts deal with challenges in the present environment that have the power to affect the quality of life of the observer or his organization. They are invariably what I call "self-defeating prophecies," for they are intended, in addition to being true accounts of what the forecasters believe they have found, to stimulate action to prevent the outcome forecasted—for example the Club of Rome's *Limits to Growth* study.

- *Secondary forecasts*, which are conditional predictions based on what would occur if certain intervening actions were taken to change the course of events projected in the primary forecasts. Instead of dealing with challenges, the focus is on possibilities that could be achieved through intervening plans of action. I call secondary forecasts "self-fulfilling prophecies," for one of their purposes is to stimulate a desired action of intervention to minimize or resolve the challenge or issue—for example Herman Kahn's *The Next Two Hundred Years*, which was written in response to the future as seen in *Limits to Growth*.

- *Tertiary forecasts*, which are conditional predictions based

---

[2]B. de Jouvenel, *The Art of Conjecture* (New York: Basic Books, 1967).

on the supposed behavior of issue champions (for example activists and special interest groups) or authorities with power to act in the legislative, regulatory, economic, technological, or social arenas. Tertiary forecasts are historical, an assumption as to what the forecasters believe people in authority will do, whereas the two other types of forecasts are estimates of what could happen in certain situations.

These types of forecasts are not in rank order but in chronological order in the issues management process; that is, a primary forecast must be in hand before a secondary one can be constructed.

Additionally, in the business world only economists and a few other hardy souls in strategic planning departments label their forecasts "forecasts." Most issues managers use other terms—environmental analysis, situational analysis, cross-impact analysis, issue briefs, or issue backgrounders. There are good and sufficient reasons for this behavior, the most important being survival, but it is only necessary that this fact be noted here. Nevertheless, issues managers of necessity develop primary and secondary forecasts in their work and somewhere along the line a tertiary forecast is involved, either formally or informally, by the managers who design the tactics to implement the issue strategy.

Bertrand de Jouvenel's definition, "forecasting consists of passing from knowledge about present conditions to estimates of future conditions," implies two separate activities: induction (fact finding) as to the present situation and deduction (forecasting proper) as to possible future conditions logically arrived at by applying our knowledge of causes and their consequences to our understanding of current facts.

FACT-FINDING TECHNIQUES

Scanning, monitoring, and networking are probably the most widely used fact-finding techniques.

Scanning is a technique for identifying an emerging issue, trend, or potentially major development as early as possible. This technique should be more properly called "media scanning," since the various media—print, electronic, film—are the subject matter scanned.

The rationale behind a systematic scanning of the media is that issues of substance aren't generated spontaneously but start off as ideas expressed first in obscure books, journals, newsletters, or other print media, sometimes as commentary on current events, sometimes as proposals. For example, the first proposals for workers' compensation and no-fault insurance appeared in academic journals. But such proposals did not leap into the public arena until several years later. These issue ideas are later taken up by special interest groups and moved into the public forums. The media in which an issue is first reported generally tells how far along the issue has advanced in its life cycle. For example, an issue that first appears in a scholarly journal is generally in its infancy. By the time it is noted in TV news or daily newspapers, it is generally well along in its development.

The American Council of Life Insurance was the first to create a broad-based and systematized media scanning process. Its Trend Analysis Program (TAP), more than 10 years old, uses volunteers from member insurance companies to scan more than 100 publications for issues, trends, and developments in the sociopolitical and economic environments of potential significance to the industry. Today, other professional and trade associations have similar systems. Corporations have their own specialized scanning processes, usually organized by their issues management staffs and supplemented through the purchase of outside scanning services, such as HRN's IssueTrack.

Monitoring is the process of tracking trends and issues identified through scanning or some other process. It is a process of systematically following the development of an issue or trend, using more selective media and intelligence-gathering methods. It can involve field trips, opinion sampling, technical research, and networking with other parties equally interested in the issue.

Scanning is thought of as a 360-degree radar sweep to search for the earliest warning of a previously unknown challenge; monitoring is described as the process of locking onto to an identified challenge and tracking its approach and the nature of its development. The process of monitoring an issue can also result in spotting a new issue or an old issue transformed into another kind of challenge.

For example, issues managers who monitored the progress of the equal pay for equal work issue, which many thought had been resolved by federal law, saw the first signs of this issue expanded to the concept of equal pay for jobs of equal worth in the literature of the women's movement. At first, a few managers didn't note the significance of the shift from "work" to "worth" and the birth of the new issue until it was renamed "comparable worth." However, even if their own internal scanning and analysis had not picked this up, use of outside scanning and social research services on a regular basis, such as IssueTrack or other services that report on opinion changes in thought-leader groups, would have given an early alert to those issues managers. Likewise, continuous content analysis of major national media as supplied by John Merram's newsletter "Issues Management Letter" or one of John Naisbitt's publications gives supplementary support to an organization's monitoring process.

Networking is the formal and informal sharing of issue information by issues managers and planners through their trade and professional associations. Core issues are covered for industry-specific issues through committees in trade associations; broader environmental issues are covered either through professional associations, such as the Issues Management Association, the American Bar Association, the American Medical Association and the Public Relations Society of America, or through regional issues networks, whose members include issues managers from many industries.

These and similar fact-finding techniques are preliminary to the development of forecasts.

FORECASTING TECHNIQUES

Although more than 150 forecasting techniques have been developed, according to a survey conducted by one futures think tank, only 8 or 10 are actually used by corporate issues managers.

Trend extrapolation is the most widely used forecasting technique because of its simplicity. This technique involves the charting of a factor or variable over time to the present and then projecting the line into the future as a continuation of the direction indicated by its most recent inflection point. Used in an uncritical fashion, this method can be dangerous, especially the further it is pushed into the future. Unless other limiting or controlling factors are taken into account, pure trend extrapolation gives an exponential curve, whereas experience has shown that the behavior of almost all systems manifests an S-curve, reflecting a slow start, exponential growth, then a leveling off as determined by some limit imposed by the environment.

An example of a corporate public policy decision based on trend extrapolation would be Allstate Insurance Company's decision to support the government's passive restraint standard for private passenger cars. In the early 1970s, Allstate's Safety Division analysts made a trend extrapolation of the current number of highway deaths, then more than 50,000 annually, through 1980. The result was a forecast that more than 500,000 people would die in highway accidents between 1970 and 1980 and about 10 million injuries would be suffered.

Factoring in the number of lives that could be saved and injuries prevented by the use of the DOT's Standard 208, the air bag/air belt requirement, the trend forecast indicated that these losses could be cut by a third to a half beginning in the late 1970s. Allstate's CEO used this and other information in making his decision to mount a public advocacy campaign in support of air bags in 1971.

Trend impact analysis (TIA) is an analytic process developed by the Futures Group to overcome the limitations of straight trend extrapolation. It divides the task of trend extrapolation between humans and computers. First, the computer extrapolates the history of a trend, then an expert or group of experts lists future events that would impact the extrapolation. The computer applies these impact judgments to modify the trend extrapolated until a satisfactory forecast is arrived at.

A similar forecasting system, called INTERAX, has been developed by the Institute for the Future. TIA, INTERAX, and other such programs have been developed for use in both strategic planning and issues management and are used by various organizations, which either have futures research think tanks contract to do the forecast or do it internally, using the procedures and software developed by the think tanks.

Delphi forecasting has been used for forecasting since the RAND Corporation developed it in the 1960s. It can be used under rigorous procedures or more loosely in an almost informal manner.

The technique is designed to improve the use of expert opinion through polling based on three conditions: anonymity of the participants' answers, statistical display of the results, and feedback of the participants' reasoning (especially for answers outside the group norm). Polling is generally conducted by mail.

An electronic device called the Concensor can produce an "instant" Delphi at a meeting with all participants present, simultaneously computing each participant's prediction and giving it a weight based on the participant's estimate of his or her own expertise, probability, and other factors.

Delphis can be used to predict the occurrence of specific events or to identify new issues and trends.

For example, the Center for Futures Research at The University of California at Los Angeles has conducted many forecasts for industries on a syndicated basis, using Delphi forecasting based on expert opinion found within the industry. When the center conducted a long-range forecast of the life insurance industry several years ago, the demise or transformation of the whole life insurance contract was clearly foreseen and substitute products were proposed from the Delphi.

Cross-impact analysis was developed as a technique to make an assessment of the interaction between trends and estimates of future events developed through Delphis and other studies. This analysis is done by assuming a trend will continue. By the use of a matrix, the analyst then tries to determine how the occurrence of that event would affect the probability and timing of other events. Cross-impact analysis is sometimes done by issues managers manually—with a pencil and paper—or electronically with computer models.

An example of computer-assisted capacity in this kind of analysis can be seen in the Center for Futures Research model. It can handle 120 trends and up to 80 events in one cross-impact analysis and forecast. This model was used in a recent Pentagon-sponsored study of the type of officers the U.S. armed forces would need in the future.

Computer simulations are mathematical models of some system, such as a corporation or a national economy. They can be induced to make forecasts when fed data about current trends and events.

Many companies have econometric models of their industry and can make complex projections about the future impact of their own or their competitors' possible actions, specific events, and so on. Although these models are used mainly by strategic planners, they are available for use by issues managers in the company. For example, at Allstate issue subcommittees have the corporate model available for reference. However, most of these econometric models are not useful in sociopolitical forecasting.

Systems dynamic modeling, as developed by Jay Forrester of the Massachusetts Institute of Technology, does have major application to the types of forecasting issues managers do. While econometric modeling is based on economic equations and various formulas, systems dynamic modeling first identifies and analyzes the system (company, environment, and so on) in question, then creates a model specific to that environment for purposes of forecasting the future effect of interactions between trends and issues within the model. Some companies use simplified software packages to do their own systems dynamic forecasting; others contract out more complex forecasting projects.

An example of the valuable use of a systems dynamic model forecast can be found in a 1979 future transition study by Jack B. Homer of the Systems Dynamics Group at MIT. The study examined the implications for insurance companies of community aging in formerly upper-class inner suburbs. It resulted in the identification of community and business policy actions that would make insurance company withdrawal unnecessary over time.

Technology assessment is a forecasting technique that develops logical, quantified predictions as to the timing and character of changes of the technical parameters in a specific field or industry. Although it was developed for other purposes, some issues managers use TA in their work, especially those in manufacturing businesses. However, issue managers in service industries will begin to incorporate this technique into their forecasting arsenal as technical issues gain greater impact in their business environments.

Technology assessment was used by Allstate in 1975 during

the first energy crisis to determine whether its public policy support of air bags should be continued. Independent automotive engineers were hired to assess the impact on automobile design and safety of the government's energy efficiency regulations. Their analysis correctly forecast that the weight of U.S.-made autos would have to be reduced, resulting in a downsizing of the cars and a serious reduction of passenger compartment space. This reduction in space placed front-seat passengers closer to the dashboard and windshields, increasing the likelihood of serious injuries to unrestrained passengers in frontal crashes. Allstate made the public policy decision to continue its support of passive restraints and to redouble its efforts to make it an advocacy goal of the entire property/casualty insurance industry because of the increased loss implications. This occurred, and advocacy leadership was taken up by the trade associations and other companies.

(This advocacy is interesting. Although Allstate began its advocacy in support of air bags in the early 1970s when all the technology was available and tested and could have been placed in most new cars by 1974, it will be early in the 21st century before most cars have them. Another force, which sociologists call the "cultural lag," has controlled the new technology. Cultural lag in our society has always been about 30 years, from the time a new procedure, system, or process is developed and the time it finally spreads throughout society.)

Scenario writing as a forecasting tool has been around since the 1950s, when the RAND Corporation first adapted it to this purpose. Herman Kahn was one of the masters of this tool.

Scenarios are chronological "histories' written from the present into the future. Many consulting organizations have developed guides on how to construct them. An inexpensive guide is available from the United Way of America. It is based on the SRI International model and was developed by United Ways' Environmental Scanning Committee.

Royal Dutch Shell has been a major user of scenario forecasting. Its *scenario forcasting* system was developed by Pierre Wack and Ted Newland, who are now independent consultants to multinational corporations in the United States and the United Kingdom. For example, through his scenario forecasting experiments Wack was able to predict the OPEC oil crisis several years in advance of its occurrence in 1974.

Scenario forecasting on a nation-state basis is done by two interesting European groups that conduct syndicated studies for corporations. These studies go beyond political risk analysis. Societie XA of Paris has conducted major studies of a number of countries. Its study of Colombia a few years back forecast many of the events now occurring there involving the government, leftist guerrillas, and drug overlords. Its study of the United States conducted in advance of the 1984 presidential election was interesting because of its analysis of the so-called military-industrial complex here. On the other hand, an interdisciplinary study conducted by faculty at Oxford through its consulting firm, Oxford Analytica Ltd., in 1984 focused on broader socioeconomic issues. Both of these forecasts, although not accurate predictions, offered American issues managers rich insights because they were made by native French and British analysts viewing the United States from their own cultural bases.

The major value of scenario writing is to let a company consider a number of possible futures in sufficient time to plan for those they think most probable. Scenario packaging is the best method issues managers have found to date to get the issues, trends, and implications in a comprehensive but compact way before their senior officers. Also, in corporations where senior management tolerates "no negative thinking" by managers and staff alike, balanced minds can get senior management to consider negative implications of policy programs with alternative scenarios, including "worst-case" scenarios, without getting fired or being tagged as "negative thinkers."

USE OF TRADE ASSOCIATIONS AND MEMBERSHIP FOR FORECASTING

Since many companies cannot afford to provide internal staffing for broad-based issue forecasting, many trade and business associations have stepped in to provide this service. In associations that have developed systems to do this, the stimulus to create this industry capability usually came from the leading company members that had already developed their own capability, and saw value in expanding it to deal with industrywide matters.

As noted earlier, one of the most noteworthy and longest-running foresight systems has been the American Council of Life Insurance's Trend Analysis Programs (TAP).

Member-company personnel are involved for both input and evaluation of trends, forecasts, and implications. Professional staff both contribute and manage the process. Outside experts are also hired when they have special expertise, unique analysis techniques, and proven forecasting skills.

It is useful to examine a typical product of ACLI's TAP program. Trend Analysis Program Report No. 28, *Haves and Have-Nots: Some Reflections* (1985) provides an excellent example of trend extrapolation, scenario writing, and cross-impact analysis. The report is based on a study of whether the middle class is disappearing in the United States because of structural-sectoral economic changes, as well as because of changes in social values.

Trend Extrapolation

Abstracts submitted by TAP monitors during 1984 highlighted an emerging debate as to whether the middle class was disappearing in this country.

When the detailed 1982 family income data became available in 1985, a 10-year trend was clear: Households with pretax incomes of between $15,000 and $35,000 declined from 51 percent of all households in 1973 to 44 percent in 1982—a drop of nearly 14 percent. However, the exodus from the middle class was bimodal. Some households dropped toward the poverty line, while nearly an equal number climbed upward into the more affluent income classes.

Even though the latest data available reflected the impact of a three-year recession (1980–1982), this trend obviously had longer-term implications.

The ACLI decided to hire an outside economist to further analyze the trend. His analysis of the 10-year period resulted in the conclusion that the middle class was *not* disappearing since the bulk of Americans still enjoy middle-class or above incomes. However, his analysis of income trends indicated that the distribution of income in American society has become more polarized. A Federal Reserve Board study showed that the most affluent 10 percent of families had 29 percent of total national income in 1969, and 33 percent in 1983. A Census Bureau statistical study showed that the poorest 20 percent of householders now have 4.7 percent of total personal income, the lowest share since 1961, three years before the massive War on Poverty began. The causes of this polarization trend were identified by the TAP team as (1) the Reagan administration's policy of shifting the tax burden away from the affluent, thereby reducing income transfer payments to the poor; (2) demographic changes, such as women entering the labor force, growth in female-headed and single-parent households, and the influx of the baby boom generation into the work force; and (3) labor-market changes, owing to our shift to a service economy, the competitive global economy, and structurally polarized jobs in the high-technology fields.

Since these causes can be expected to have an impact for the next decade or longer, the TAP report concluded that this trend toward greater income inequality will continue.

Scenario

On the basis of this trend analysis, ACLI staff constructed the following scenario of the likely future:

Some people will see their earnings and discretionary incomes soar to new heights. Baby boomers who form two-career households, older Americans with substantial retirement incomes, and some professional minorities and women will form a new class of affluents. These new affluents will be great consumers of luxury items, expensive vacations, and lavish homes. This group of Americans will also be privy to the best health-care services, financial advice, investment opportunities, and services for their dependents.

Increasing polarization of income suggests continuing erosion of living standards for millions of Americans. The federal government, in turning its attention to resolving the hugh deficit in the years ahead, will have neither the means nor the disposition to expand poverty programs. The poorest of the poor will face dire economic problems in the coming year.

Perhaps more important is the growing number of Americans who were once among the middle class and now are finding themselves living nearer the poverty line. These Americans— blue-collar laborers in declining industries, families that lose their farms due to debt and decreasing governmental subsidies, divorced women with children, and the aged solely dependent on social security—will make up the "new poor."

Cross-Impact Analysis

The TAP report concludes with a cross-impact analysis of these trends on the life insurance industry. Because the report was intended for general guidance of members of an industry, the cross-impacts were not presented in a chart form, but in a narrative form with leading questions to assist company planners who must develop specific responses to the trends.

Projecting the trends gives greater market segmentation for the industry, for they imply a growing market of affluent and sophisticated consumers of financial products. (It is estimated that there are now 1 million millionaires in the United States.) The trends also imply a growing low-income market, which can least afford the normal costs of risk protection insurance provides. Because both of these markets are growing faster than the life insurance industry's traditional middle-class market, income polarization is perceived as the key "driving" trend for the future of the life insurance industry.

The impact of the "new affluents"—two-career baby boom couples and young single professionals—relates to their insurance and financial needs, which will change over their careers. Income protection is perceived by those couples as a major need in the event of the early death of one of the members; over time, however, the protection and growth of their estate will become of paramount importance, as will retirement income planning. What new products will be needed to meet the needs of this part of the financial market? How can the life insurance industry better compete with other financial services to maintain its market position with these new affluents as they age and seek greater asset-building and retirement-financing products? Will the sales to the new affluents offset or more than offset the drop in sales to the middle class?

The impact of members falling from the middle class to the low-income class will cause increasing replacements of existing life policies to lower premium and lower death benefit policies, as well as increasing lapses in premium payments on current policies. What new, low-cost insurance products can be developed to protect these households? What new financial planning services at affordable costs can be developed for this market? What new cost-effective delivery mechanisms and sales processes need to be developed to meet the requirements of this growing low-income market? What public policy issues will emerge out of the newly perceived needs of the new poor?

The income polarization trend also will impact the future state of group policies, according to the TAP report. The new dual economy can be epitomized by the service economy in which new companies are formed, creating new jobs with small numbers of highly paid executives at one end and large numbers of employees earning slightly above the minimum wage at the other end. Thus, new group policy packages will have to be developed to interest companies with this kind of extreme dual-pay scale.

Public policy impact questions raised in the report include: How will regional poverty problems affect life insurance company investments in those areas? Will declining household incomes have an impact on life expectancy?

It should be noted that this TAP report was based on current data revealing the polarization of *household incomes* and its impact on the middle class. The TAP report was published shortly before a Bureau of Labor Statistics study of middle income *jobs* was issued. The BLS study revealed that there was a relative *stability* of *middle-income jobs* during the same period of the TAP study, 1973–1982. The TAP study would be further enriched by incorporation of these data, although the middle-income jobs data do not contradict the middle-income household data. They merely indicate that complex social and family-value shifts begun in the late 1960s and early 1970s are working their way through society now.

Note that this TAP report is a general forecast packaged in a brief form (19 pages of text) for the general guidance of member life insurance companies. Strategic planners and issues managers in the member companies who wish to use the TAP report to plan aggressively for the future of their corporations might integrate other information they have, expand the analysis, and then focus on high-priority business and public policy matters related to their respective companies.

THE ART OF FORECASTING

Although many of the forecasting techniques now used involve mathematical extrapolations, statistical manipulations, and so on, a survey of issues managers by Joe Coates & Associates in Washington, D.C., found that there are few applications for mathematical extrapolations in issues management. The reason is that issues managers deal more with sociopolitical forecasting than with numbers-based economic forecasting. Sociopolitical forecasting is still an art, not a science. And critics point out that economic forecasting is also an art, not a science, when forecasts and results are compared.

In the end, in the world of affairs and application, all of the professions, regardless of the scientific tools available to them, are arts. This is true of surgeons as well as business managers, including issues managers. We never have absolute knowledge of the facts before we must make decisions. We must make decisions on the basis of informed judgment only. Issues managers use their knowledge, experience, and skills to help senior management develop the best informed judgments possible under current circumstances. The use of forecasting techniques is central to the process.

Information has always been a major strategic resource of successful companies. Good forecasting practices enrich the existing information base and expand its value as a strategic resource.

CHAPTER NINE

Developing Corporate Policy

Policy making by high-level government officials is literally a science, supported by extensive guidelines, research literature, and professional academic programs.

Policy making by high-level corporate executives is currently an intuitive art at best. The difference is due to the academic and professional training each type of officials receives and the career paths each type pursues.

However, the picture is changing in the corporate world, due primarily to the emergence of strategic planning and issues management concepts and practices. The extensive literature and academic programs in our business schools based on strategic planning systems guarantee a steady infusion into the corporate world of managers conscious of business policy. The same is occurring for future issues managers in the area of corporate public policy matters, as more university business and public relations schools are developing curriculums for this management discipline.

Despite these developments, little specific attention is devoted to methods for developing corporate policy itself. Both strategic planning and issues management systems require policy making or reassessment at one or more stages in their processes. But none I have examined deals in depth with the matter. This chapter is devoted to my understanding of how corporate policy is made in the new environment, based on my observations of senior officers within several corporations and industry groups dominated by corporate CEOs, as well as my own contributions to the process as a staff manager and policy resource person.

CORPORATE POLICY

Corporate policy in modern practice is simply the statement of a corporation's commitment to a high-level goal or goals, expressing or implying the acceptable procedures the company will use in achieving them. Older usages of the term in governmental policy making also included concepts of both a high-level commitment to goals *and* plans to achieve them. Policy setting for goals in corporate practice is separate from planning action programs to support them.

Thus, a corporate policy identifies the lodestar, the corporate goal, on which all managers' compasses should be fixed. Planning and charting the path toward the goal is a function of the corporate planning systems that generate both long- and short-range plans. However, policy setting and communication is the only mechanism available to a large corporation to keep both management and operations in sync.

Throughout the history of every corporation, policies have guided the management team. Furthermore, for most of this century (until the last decade or so), these policies have primarily been unwritten or, when written, have been only partial statements of the larger understood policy. This situation had one major advantage: It allowed for elbow room and the right to act creatively in executing the understood policy. It had many disadvantages, the main one being that understood policy made it difficult to discipline managers who deviated from it in daily operations or who decided to quietly change it to their personal or departmental advantage and to the ultimate disadvantage of the company.

When giant corporations emerged and the King-Kong-sized conglomerates appeared, made up of many separate companies, the enormous task of managing resulted in serious efforts to set high-level policies in writing, with procedural rules. Thick policy manuals and thicker operating procedures manuals were inserted into the structure. Although studied carefully by managers when first issued, the policy manuals soon moved off their desks to gather dust on credenzas. Policies that were not part of the corporate culture and intuitively understood by the managers never saw the light of day in practice. They were observed or consulted only in the breech. (Managers consult policy manuals only when they get into trouble to see if the manuals contain language permitting exotic interpretations or pleas of extenuating circumstances to cover their mistakes.)

Although a number of companies during the past 10 years have made efforts to put all major policies into written statements, the enormity of the task has defeated most of these efforts. I was once asked to examine the feasibility of reducing all major public policies to written form for one company. Research revealed that the task would not have been cost effective. More important, in that company it would also have seriously disrupted operations. The managers were constantly changing the form of their understanding of the policy to solve current problems while trying to remain faithful to its substance. This fact contributed to the company's success. But senior management discovered that the situation was permitting junior managers to set new policy on the scene, usurping senior management's function. Management moved to the system described below.

A few companies have followed the practice of formalizing their major policies in writing at each stage of their development, to guide not only current management but future management as well. These few companies can be identified by their continuously successful performance over the years and the continuity of their corporate identity. However, the vast majority of companies have not done this. Their main recourse for the future lies in moving older unwritten and newly needed policies to writing through the normal operation of their strategic planning and issues management processes. This permits the development of strategies and programs each function is responsible for executing so that the whole organization can arrive at each successive goal as one powerful unit.

POLICY MANAGEMENT

Although it has been known for many years that one of the ways to manage large organizations is through policy-setting techniques, there has been little discussion in the business world of the concept of managing policy making itself, as well as policy execution.

The first person to advance this concept was W. Howard Chase, who was also the first to define the concept of issue management and pioneer the development of its theory. In a remarkably insightful article, "The Corporate Imperative: Management of Profit and Policy" (published in the *Corporate Public Issues* newsletter of March 1, 1982), Chase proposed that the corporation of the future will be reorganized into two main functions. The corporate organization chart he proposed has one function headed "public policy management" and another labeled "profit management."

In support of senior management's goal of strategically managing the whole corporation in its sociopolitical and economic environments, Chase calls for each function to be guided by a strategic policy planning (issues management) system or a strategic profit planning (business) system. Although this proposal has been debated on its merits, the important point to note is that it is but another expression of Chase's decades of experience in the business world. He argued before and in this proposal that policy making itself can be managed and that the implementation of policy can be managed, but that they are two separate functions. I agree. The current assumption that policy making is merely a step in the planning process underestimates its critical importance to the entire process. Policy doesn't spring automatically from the facts at hand. It is created and fitted to the needs of the corporation. It is much more complex and critical in any planning process than planners presently acknowledge. It is worthy of its own methodology.

Another recognition of the need of policy management emerged in a governmental context several years before Chase's articulation of it in the business world. In the United Kingdom, newly appointed Prime Minister Edward Heath created the Central Policy Review Staff in 1970. This group served his office and his newly appointed cabinet made up of members of the Conservative party. According to Lord Hunt, CPRS's mission was to fill "the hole in the centre" of British government, the policy hole. Heath's purpose when assuming the prime ministership was to retain a capability he and his shadow cabinet had when they were in the opposition: to consider policy and strategy as a whole and to take a long-term view of things. Heath noted that when the opposition took over the government, it proved impossible to do that under the press of circumstances. He ordered the creation of a staff unit that would provide that capability continuously. CPRS was the result.

Its charter, as stated in a White Paper, said: "Governments are always at some risk of losing sight of the need to consider the totality of their current policies in relation to their longer term objectives; and . . . of evaluating . . . the alternative policy options and priorities open to them." CPRS, known as the "Think Tank," worked on scores of high-priority issues and policy matters. One of its first projects in 1970 was the study of energy issues. It forecast a steep price rise of oil in 1971, well ahead of the Arab-Israeli War in 1973 and OPEC's subsequent price cartel, and recommended measures to counteract that possibility.

CPRS was concerned with the balance of policy, that is, the way the government's programs fitted into its strategic objectives and the way it was ordering its priorities. CPRS lasted 13 years through both Conservative and Labor governments. After her reelection in 1983, Margaret Thatcher disbanded CPRS, stating that the purposes for which it was established were being handled in other ways. One member of Parliament commented on her action: "She cannot see an institution without hitting it with her handbag." However another commentator gave a more likely explanation: CPRS staff was too vigorous in rubbing her ministers' noses into the future.[1]

Although CPRS issued a number of public reports, details of its procedures, methods, and studies will not be public for a number of years under British law. It is important to note, however, that this 13-year operation was the first large-scale and reasonably successful effort at both the management of policy and its implementation with professional staff support.

Heath's creation of the Central Planning Review Staff in 1970 was his response to the recognition that "a hole existed in the centre of government." American corporate CEOs created strategic planning and issues management staffs in the late

---

[1] C. Hennessy, S. Morrison, and R. Townsend, *Strathclyde Papers on Government and Politics No. 31* (Glasgow U.K.: University of Strathclyde, 1984).

1970s in response to the same problem: recognition that a "major policy hole existed in the center of corporations." Both resulted in the evolution of the concept of policy management.

SETTING POLICY

Policy is never made in a vacuum. Even in companies that have few formal written policies, corporate maxims, mottoes, and slogans exist, whether expressed in advertisements or executive speeches, on brand labels, or mounted in wall plaques. Every company has a history and corporate culture that has grown up within it. Policy making must initially conform to that history and culture, unless it is announced to be a specific break from them as new conditions and new goals require.

The creation of policy always encompasses these elements:

- High-level goals.
- Moral (normative) as well as business (objective) standards.
- Stakeholder recognition.
- Management commitment.

Regardless of any earlier policy statements, the mission statement developed to guide the strategic planning and issues management processes takes precedence over them. The mission statement is the master policy senior management has set for the corporation. It is also an expression of management's understanding of the charter it holds in existing to serve its stakeholders.

The mission statement given below is typical of those adopted by contemporary corporations (although some companies express their mission by listing company goals):

> To provide those publics, whom we can best serve, products and services which are responsive to need and delivered at the lowest possible cost consistent with a financial return that will ensure customer satisfaction, corporate continuity, growth, and employee opportunity. We will fulfill our social and citizenship responsibilities to the greatest extent possible consistent with our financial integrity and a high level of corporate ethics. We will provide high standards of product quality and service to our customers as we maintain a leadership role in our industry. We will keep our organization growing and thereby provide addi-

tional opportunities for our employees regardless of their sex, race, religion, or ethnic background. And we will earn a profit adequate to provide the capital to accomplish all the objectives and to pay dividends to our stockholders so they receive a reasonable rate of return on their investment.

Note that the mission statement sets forth senior management's vision for the corporation, its business and social goals, its ethical and moral commitments, and the stakeholders it acknowledges as primary (customers, employees, shareholders, and the public). This is the company's master policy, stated in general terms so it can be clearly understood by all concerned. The master policy is also management's commitment that this mission statement will guide its actions.

Because the mission statement is the broad corporate policy, operating policies to implement it and be reflected in corporate action are needed. Usually, each functional department (marketing, production, personnel, and public relations/public affairs) constructs its own mission statement, which confirms the managers' understanding of the corporate policy and their commitment to achieve it.

Since all department heads have specific, although narrow, policy making authority, any policy they generate must conform to the company's and their department's missions.

More specific and broader interdepartmental policy is generated in the strategic planning and issues management systems the company has. Because the working committees for these systems contain representatives from all affected departments, their interests are represented. Because all policy formulations proposed by these systems are reviewed and adjusted by senior management, the coherence of company policy and direction is assured.

Thus, in the modern corporation, policy is generated in a participatory fashion, although responsibility and accountability for it remain in the hands of senior management. In the past, policy making was conceived of as the *sole* prerogative of the CEO, and woe be unto the junior officer or manager who even volunteered suggestions. Modern CEOs view team-building and getting maximum use of the corporate talent available to them superior to the maintainence of an ancient prerogative. The corporate world is a better one today because of it.

CHAPTER TEN

Senior Management and the Issues Management Staff

The success of every issues management system depends on the relationship of the organization's senior management to the issues management staff that serves it. Difficulties occur when there is a misunderstanding of the proper role each plays.

Senior officers, especially the CEO, are truly managers in the classical business definition of the term: They are responsible for the work of other people. They work through other people. In addition to organizing and directing the work of others, they have a second but equally important function: direction setting and decision making. If they are doing functional or operating department work, they are not performing as top managers. This work is done by staff and line managers.

Therefore, when senior management turns to its planning duties, be it strategic business planning or public policy (issues management) planning, a distinction should be made early between its function and the planning staff's function.

Senior management's function relates to the decision-making points in the issues management process. It makes the decisions related to the prioritization or order ranking of emerging issues selected for further research and analysis by staff and/or ad hoc issue task forces or subcommittees. It receives progress reports from staff and task forces. Finally, it receives, debates, and decides final policy positions and strategies and action programs that will support the policies. Senior management is responsible for the issues management function within the company, just as it is responsible for all high-level planning and operating functions.

The issues management staff and internal departmental managers with relevant expertise are responsible for developing all the necessary background resources necessary for senior management to meet its responsibilities. This means that staff and related groups are responsible for emerging-issue scanning and monitoring, analysis for prioritization, company impact assessments, policy options, and supporting strategies and action plans and programs capable of execution.

Although a permanent staff is required for all successful corporate issues management systems and must be housed in some departmental unit, the staff is not the company's "issues management department," since the work involves not only senior management but all other department managers, according to the issues under study. Thus, territorial boundaries are irrelevant at the staff level. Placing responsibility at the senior officer level lifts issues management out of the lower staff and operating department levels. Knowledge of this fact within the organization creates a synergy unusual for most functions—everybody "owns" a piece of the issues management process and seeks to contribute. This not only permits senior management to get an extra dividend from existing managers (more valuable work output); the process is also a companywide team-building system.

SENIOR MANAGEMENT PARTICIPANTS

In large companies, specific senior officers are assigned to direct the issues management system, either through specially created issues management committees or public issues committees. In some cases, the executive committee assumes this function. At a minimum, these committees include the COO and all senior officers responsible for the major functions. Usually, these committees include between 6 and 10 members. The senior issues management staff manager is also a member, usually as the secretary, facilitator, and resource person. However, he or she does not vote when policy decisions are made. That is senior management's responsibility. A nonvoting manager also assures other departments within the company that the senior staff manager is an objectively independent professional, carrying neither a bias in favor of one type of approach nor a brief for one of the inevitable factions that spring up inside the company over certain issues.

In smaller companies, the CEO is the senior "committee," turning to the issues management staff and trusted senior officers to perform senior management's duties after the staff work has been done.

STAFF SELECTION

Most corporations with successful issues management systems select staff from employees with relevant skills and 10 years or more of service with the company. This is done for two reasons: They already understand the company's business and management culture and they know the industry in which it operates. These employees can recognize emerging issues with potential corporate impact and possess keener insight than outsiders. However, the staff is frequently supplemented by hiring specialists from the outside (economists, sociologists, historians, social psychologists, market forecasters, and lawyers) according to need. An outside hire is never initially made the senior staff manager, because it usually takes from 12 to 24 months for a person to become fully acclimated to the company and absorb its history, value system, and so on. Over time, an outside hire sometimes rises to the senior staff management position after the individual has been fully seasoned and tested.

A few companies have brought in ex-government officers, think tank gurus, and others to set up and lead the issues management staff. Only a few of these have succeeded in earning general acceptance within the company's issues management process. They are viewed either as "troublesome" outsiders (with fear of their influence) or the "sociology department" (with humor), as a source of nice-to-know information and trivia rather than hard need-to-know information for running the company. The CEO determines how these outside hires will be perceived and accepted.

A number of failed attempts at creating an issues management system are directly attributable to incorrect selection of staff. I know of four companies that tried and failed, one company twice, because they hired recent college graduates, such as MBAs, to set up and staff the function. Since management had even less experience with a formal issues management system than the recent college graduates (who at least had course work in strategic and social policy planning), it is little wonder that failure was the result.

Those companies that established their own successful systems drew professionals from their public relations, public affairs, corporate planning, human resources, and/or marketing departments to staff their issues management operations. This kind of staff knows whether additional talent, drawn from inside or outside the corporation, is needed to make the system work.

Staff size in large companies range from 1 to 40 full-time members, according to whether the issues management staff will do the environmental analysis for the strategic planning department or government relations/public affairs department. In these companies budgets run from $50,000 to over $300,000 per year, exclusive of staff salaries.

BENEFITS

Staff size, budget, and the system's influence are totally dependent on senior management's desire for and appreciation of an issues management system. In deciding whether to institute an issues management system within a company, executives should consider the experience of one company that has long had a system in place.

Rexnord Corporation's Public Relations Vice President, David L. Shanks, has summarized the benefits this way:[1]

> There are many benefits to be derived in properly managing issues. I would like to list six of them. They are both protective and opportunistic.
>
> 1. Allows management to select issues that will have the greatest impact on the corporation.
> 2. Allows "management of" versus "reaction to" issues.
> 3. Inserts relevant issues into the strategic planning process.

---

[1]D. L. Shanks in *Organizing for Issues Management*, Proceedings of Corporate Section Session, Public Relations Society of America, San Diego, 1977, p. 48.

4.   Gives the company the ability to act in tune with society.
5.   Provides opportunities for leadership roles.
6.   Protects the credibility of business in the public mind.

Many people realize that being in tune with society may be a matter of survival. At the current rate of change, we may soon lose a great socioeconomic system unless many of us get firmly involved now.

CHAPTER ELEVEN

The Role of Advocacy Advertising in Issues Management

The news media, which play an essential role in the development of issues in the public policy arena, are independent of central government or any other control. Professional journalists hew to a long tradition that requires them to be reporters and advocates for the public. They seek to report to the public, without fear or favor, what they think the public should know about its institutions and the life about them. The First Amendment gives reporters and any other citizen the right to engage in this activity. Our democracy could not function without a free mass media; cohesion in our society of a quarter of a billion citizens would be impossible without a free press.

The mass media as a whole are our national forum. All other forums, legislatures, and public meetings pale by comparison in the formation of public opinion, national consensus, or a united will to act. Corporations and other organizations have limited access to the news and editorial columns via editors and journalists. But they can never be sure that the totality of their institutional positions and arguments will be presented during critical periods of public debate. This is because the role of a journalist requires the reporter to view all institutions and established groups in a skeptical, arms-length manner. Journalists have no responsibility to carry any organization's brief. They have only the tradition of being the champion of the underdog, of defending the unfairly treated—almost always individuals, seldom institutions.

Time and again corporations and other organizations find that their responses to charges, carefully prepared arguments in favor of one or another program to resolve critical issues, are reported in the briefest form, if reported at all. In the face of this situation, advocacy (or "issue") advertising emerged in the early 1970s to give business a voice in public policy debate. Advocacy ads appeared almost entirely in the print media, with only a few of the independent broadcast media venturing to carry them. To date, the three major television networks have barred advocacy ads because of the FTC's fairness doctrine, which interestingly enough was devised to encourage public debate. Networks feared public interest groups would require so much free equal response time to corporate advocacy ads that the costs to them would seriously weaken their financial structure, although they cloaked this fear in other terms.

As for corporations' right to speak on public issues, the Supreme Court has settled that matter once and for all. Corporations, except under certain narrow conditions, have the same First Amendment rights as do citizens and other organizations, be they political parties, unions, special interest groups, or religions (*First National Bank of Boston* v. *Bellotti*, 435 U.S. 765, 1978). Subsequent court decisions have reaffirmed this decision and clarified exceptions to the rule.

However, public interest group leaders and a few academic activists have challenged this right. They argue that the wealth of corporations is such that they could "buy" public opinion via advocacy ads in the face of their opponents' inability to be heard due to lack of money to buy similar ads. However, national surveys of public attitudes by the Opinion Research Corporation have revealed that the majority of the public does not agree with arguments against advocacy ads advanced by public interest groups.

As much as 60 percent of those questioned favored the idea of companies using paid advertising to present their viewpoints on controversial public policy issues. This survey was made in the early 1980s. A more recent survey of reporters and editors revealed that they were of the same mind, believing that corporations should use paid advertising to get their positions across rather than depending on more space in the news columns. Over two thirds of those who were aware of advocacy ads declared them to be at least fairly believable, and nearly the same number believed that the advocacy ads helped them better understand the issues involved.

Of special interest is that 60 percent of those surveyed by ORC endorsed the concept of corporate advocacy advertising, even though 64 percent acknowledged that companies using such advertising might have an unfair advantage over public interest groups because the latter have less money to spend. However, 51 percent of those interviewed felt that interest groups have an unfair advantage over corporations because of the amount of news coverage given the interest group's point of view.

Thus, the public is interested in corporations' opinions and proposed solutions to public issues and accept their right to present them.

Although image or corporate (as opposed to product) advertising has been around since the early 1900s (AT&T was an early user), strong, purposeful advocacy advertising did not come into broad use until the early 1970s. Besides Mobil, broadly recognized as the most vociferous, many other corporations with determined CEOs took to the advertising media to get their opinions to the public in an unedited form. Some of those early companies were Allstate, State Farm, Aetna, and Travelers, among insurance companies and ARCO, Conoco, Getty Oil, Phillips Petroleum, and Shell, among oil companies. Other corporate standouts were Dow, DuPont, Kaiser Aluminum, Monsanto, Consolidated Edison, United Technologies, and W. R. Grace.

Currently, W. R. Grace is the most visible in its efforts to get the federal deficit under control. Its efforts to get its messages onto network television, however, have met with the same frustration and failure that Allstate, Mobil, and others faced in the 1970s.

One of the most successful short-burst, high-intensity issue advocacy campaigns was conducted by W. R. Grace in 1978 when Congress sought to increase the capital gains tax to 52 percent, under pressure from the Carter administration. Grace's $300,000 advocacy ad campaign, "The Disincentivization of America," concentrated mainly on carefully selected newspapers. Grace succeeded in not only preventing the tax increase, but helped get the capital gains tax *reduced* to 20 percent! (Look for a major campaign to get favorable capital gains treatment into the most recent federal tax law passed in 1986.)

GUIDELINES FOR ADVOCACY AD CAMPAIGNS

The following guidelines are useful to corporations creating advocacy advertising campaigns. They are based on my own experience and knowledge of how others have developed issue ad campaigns. These steps are not necessarily in rank order but follow the chronological sequence involved.

- Commitment by the CEO to participation in public policy debates on issues affecting the company and its stakeholders.
- Identification of issues. The issues management staff is used to identify those issues of major concern that cluster about the public debate.
- Issue selection. The key question or related questions are framed in regard to the issue.
- Issue research. In addition to information collection, another type of research is necessary. Dr. Robert B. Hill, the National Urban League's research director calls this type "advocacy research." At an American Enterprise Institute forum, he has explained this approach by stating:

    We do overdocument our reports, but that is so we can always find the statistical basis for our assertions, because quite often we come up with findings that people do not exactly agree with. We feel it is important to show the statistical base for our conclusions. I must underscore that point because, although I say our research is advocacy research, and that it is value oriented, we believe that it must be scientifically acceptable.

    We accomplish this by adhering to the rigors of scientific methodology—by showing where the numbers come from and by subjecting our findings to other researchers with other value orientations. It is not incompatible to have a value-oriented approach and also scientifically acceptable procedures.[1]

- Corporate policy formation, goal setting, and internal/external program planning.
- Audience selection. Outside advertising agency help is used to supplement internal corporate judgment.

* Message selection. Pretesting by the advertising agency is essential.
* Media selection brings the process to the final budget and goal-setting stage.
* Campaign execution. This must be accompanied by intensive monitoring, especially in the early phases when adjustments can be made quickly in the message, the media schedule, and audience reach.
* Measuring performance against goals while the campaign is underway.
* Evaluation permits strategic or tactical adjustments to be made in the last stages of the campaign.

PRAGMATIC RULES

The above procedure has its own set of "rules" to keep in mind while preparing and executing a campaign:

* All advocacy campaigns must strengthen the new bottom line and represent the interest of the major corporate stakeholders. Windmills are to be admired, not attacked with corporate resources.
* If your message and your motives can be misunderstood, they will be. Bitter experiences of some companies suggest an even stronger corollary: "Even if they can't be misunderstood, they will be by your opponents."
* The CEO and the board must be ready to take heat from opponents during a public campaign. If not, the more effective your efforts, the more likely you will find yourself retiring from the field, defeat snatched from the jaws of victory, at considerable institutional expense and personal pain.
* The primary purpose of an advocacy campaign is to persuade, not merely to inform. You are entering the public policy arena, where the social control of business is effected. Public interest groups understand that politics is not merely the art of compromise, but at bottom is the art of persuasion.
* You must seek the "sale" from the persuaded. Do not disturb the public with problems unless you can propose solutions on which the public or its representatives can act. As

public relations counselor William Ruder has pointed out: "Information is passive; communication is active." A campaign is a failure if it can be classified as a NATO—no action, talk only.

* The basic financial public relations rule applies to advocacy advertising. Just as you cannot have honest stock markets without honest information on which to act, you cannot have an honest public policy process without accurate advocacy messages. Objective data must be handled scrupulously; softer information and conclusions must represent senior management's best judgment.

* Expect legal and/or regulatory maneuvers aimed at shutting down your campaign as it becomes successful. Many companies have had excellent advocacy campaigns interrupted and shut down by lawsuits or the threat of lawsuits instigated by organized professions, public interest groups, or regulators who sought to deny First Amendment rights to companies waging responsible issue advocacy campaigns.

* Messages and actions must express corporate responsibility and good will toward the public and opponents. Strident, angry, demeaning responses to opponents shift attention away from issues and solutions being offered, focusing instead on what will be perceived as the company's surly corporate countenance—to the delight of your opponents and the dismay of your supporters. Advocacy ad pretesting research has revealed that the more argumentative the message, the less persuasive it is. Thus, extreme positions should be avoided. In the spirit of reasonableness, all efforts must be directed to keeping the debate on the issue itself.

* A sense of humor helps . . .

* . . . as does faith in the democratic process.

ADVOCACY ADS EFFECTIVE AT NATIONAL AND LOCAL LEVELS

Corporate executives tend to think of using advocacy advertising only when facing national issues. But as those companies regulated at the state level know, ads are valuable tools at the state and local level too.

However, proposed legislation can move on the state level much more quickly than it can on the national level. Extreme caution should be used when considering advocacy ads while state legislatures are in session. This author has seen an entire industry's lobbying effort fail because of an advocacy ad run by one company in that industry, watching angry legislators' waving the ad above their heads on the floor of the chamber, stampeding a negative vote.

For further discussion of other implications of the use of advocacy advertising in the issues management process, see Robert L. Heath and Richard Alan Nelson, *Issues Management: Corporate Public Policymaking in an Information Society* (Beverly Hills, Calif.: Sage Publications, 1986) and my article, "Advocacy Advertising: The Voice of Business in Public Policy Debate," *Public Affairs Review*, vol. III, 1982, the Journal of the Public Affairs Council.

CHAPTER TWELVE

Issues Management in Action: Cases

Issues management systems have been operating in major corporations as conscious public policy foresight, planning, and management techniques for 10 years now. Early ones were narrow, loosely structured, and involved only one or two officers and part-time staff. Results were sufficiently gratifying, and the need for a formal system with full-time staff was recognized.

Two problems face an outside investigator when trying to gather examples of real-world corporate issues and their resolution. First, the normal effect of a smooth-running issues management system within a company results in the anticipation and *avoidance* of internal and external issue confrontations, leaving the investigator looking for crises that simply didn't occur. The very success of the system by its nature produces no dramas of the Wagnerian type. In this regard, the system is doing what it is supposed to do. The company using it experiences this, but outsiders trying to decide whether the system is for them are left with little by which to judge its merits.

Second, the most dramatic and critically important issue resolutions resulting from many companies' issues management work are never publicly revealed. This results from two concerns.

First, knowledge of the nature of the issue and how it was resolved involve proprietary matters, which would be of considerable advantage to competitors and disadvantage to the company that successfully handled it. Second, the manner in which the issue was resolved appeared to be due to the leadership of other actors, not the company, although the solution, strategy, and players' roles were created within the company's issues management group. Revealing the company's role and how the resolution was achieved, even though highly ethical methods were used, would be neither politic nor diplomatic—and could possibly create a new issue of another order of complexity. In addition, some issues—especially those dealing with unauthorized or independent actions of employees, real or merely perceived to be occurring—are sometimes too sensitive to publicly acknowledge, even within the company community. The issues management system is used to quietly analyze the matter, then effect a resolution without fanfare. Bendix Corporation's senior management would have greatly benefited from this kind of tool several years ago.

It would perhaps be instructive to see how a well-meaning company got into serious difficulties because it did not have an issues management system, and also to examine how it ameliorated the consequences by adopting an issues management system to wind the matter down.

HOOKER CHEMICAL

The names of Hooker Chemical and Love Canal are inextricably linked in the annals of corporate responsibility or, in the public's mind, of corporate irresponsibility. The record is interesting and the public's perception is incorrect.

Hooker's management was diligent in deciding how to dispose of toxic wastes produced at its manufacturing sites during the 1940s and 1950s. When Hooker bought the nearby abandoned Love Canal bed in the Niagara Falls area, management researched state and federal regulations regarding storage of such wastes—and then went further. Next, it consulted with the scientific community on the best way to store the chemicals to protect the public. Management complied with every known regulation at the time, using the best information and techniques available, to seal the bottom, sides, and ends of the canal.

By the early 1950s, Hooker had filled up the canal, permanently sealed off the top with nonpermeable clay, and topped that off with soil, grass, plants, and shrubbery. The company wanted to be a good neighbor and a responsible corporate citizen. It intended to always maintain ownership of the land and not to sell it or build on it, for management knew the dangers of breaking the clay seal topping.

The original public issue had to do with a community relations problem frequently faced by corporations. In 1952 the Niagara Falls board of education wanted Hooker's "unused" land, the Love Canal toxic waste dump, for a new school site to accommodate the community's post-World War II baby boomers.

Hooker executives were horrified and explained both privately and at public hearings why the site was unsuitable for any kind of building or human habitation. The school board grew adamant. The community and local media sided with the board and began to view Hooker as a selfish corporation for resisting.

Next, the school board threatened condemnation proceedings. Until this time, Hooker had always been considered locally as a good corporate citizen. Management decided it should avoid the adversarial proceedings, with its potential for worsening relations within the community. But it first insisted that the school board agree that any school would be built on top of the ground, without basements, and that the unused land would never be sold for residential construction. The school board officials agreed, according to Hooker, but the verbal agreement was never reduced to a written contract.

In 1953, Hooker sold the Love Canal site for $1, and the school board agreed in the sales contract to assume "all risk and liability." This without doubt was the worst public transaction in the history of any American corporation, although made from the best of motives.

At first, the school board was mindful of Hooker's warnings. The school was built adjacent to the toxic dump site, the site used merely as a playground. Land speculators and home builders began to covet the open land around the school at Love Canal. The school district began to experience financial difficulties.

Despite Hooker's warnings about breaking the clay cap encasing the dump site, the school board leased some of the land for development and allowed some of the top soil to be taken for landfill and foundations to be dug for the homes. Hooker protested vigorously to the school board and the public. Finally, when sewers were dug in the canal in 1957, penetrating the clay cap, Hooker ran ads in local newspapers warning the public about the dangers involved in building homes on the Love Canal site. Hooker's public campaign was ignored and then forgotten by residents.

In 1968, 15 years after the sale of the dump site to the school board, the New York State highway department constructed a new expressway, cutting through the southwestern tip of the canal, thereby *opening* one end of the formerly sealed canal. When record rainfalls hit in 1976, the toxic chemicals in Love Canal were washed into the community, filling basements and saturating nearby homesites.

Hooker offered on its own to pay one third of the estimated $850,000 cleanup costs, even though it had no legal liability under its sale contract. However, the city was unable to come up with the balance, and the plan fell through. The national media picked up the story. Over the next two years, Hooker found itself the scapegoat in what became a national scandal.

During the early period of building at the landsite, Hooker discovered that as membership changed regularly on the school board, new members rejected any understanding of the land sale transaction that no ground-penetrating building would take place on the Love Canal site because the agreement had not been reduced to writing in contract form.

If Hooker had had a public policy foresight and planning system in place, instead of the traditional public relations/public affairs firefighting council it apparently used in 1953, most if not all of the future damage could have been avoided. Elementary long-term analysis and scenarios would have revealed that Hooker could never *voluntarily* give up physical control of the dump site, given its knowledge of what would happen if the clay seals were ever broken. Therefore, in 1953, it had but one choice: force the school district to commence condemnation proceedings during which Hooker could make the scientific and practical case for severe restrictions on future use of the site.

Then, even if the school district had prevailed, a court would have retained jurisdiction and would have placed permanent restrictions on the type of building that could take place at the site. It would have had the power to enforce those restrictions even if future school board members decided to act otherwise.

Although irreparable damage to the community and company's reputation had been done, Hooker decided in 1979 that it had to assume leadership in resolving the issue. It hired an experienced public relations agency, Daniel J. Edelmen, Inc., and organized an internal issues group to focus on Love Canal problems. By 1982, the Environmental Protection Agency issued a report finding that Hooker had effectively contained the central dump site and that the area was as habitable now as the rest of Niagara Falls.

The sad consequences of Hooker's reluctant, but voluntary, acquiescence to the local school district is that the community, the state, and the nation will jointly bear the inevitable costs of the original decision. The U.S. Office of Technology Assessments estimates that the bill will be enormous: $2 million to dispose of the wastes properly, $100 million to clean up the site, and $2 billion in the settlement of pending lawsuits.

The only lesson that can be learned from this case is that when an issues management system is not in place early, it still has value in organizing the longer-term corporate response in winding down the painful and damaging results in a rational and responsive manner.

A TOXIC CHEMICAL CASE WITH A HAPPIER ENDING

American Can Company's issues management experience in connection with a major public health issue is enlightening, because it represents an issue initiative on the company's part.

Frank J. Connor, the company's president and chief operating officer, gave this account before the Issues Management Association of why his company adopted an issues management process:

> The time available for making decisions is growing shorter and shorter, and the stakes, bigger and bigger. Technological, economic, and social changes are happening faster. And a company can no longer comfort itself that 10 or 12 digits of assets will carry it through. The railroads thought that, Detroit thought it, so did the textile, rubber, shipbuilding, steel, and retailing industries.
>
> American Can was like many companies in those industries. So it might be instructive to recount some of the issues it faced in transforming itself, in less than four years, from a successful but threatened dinosaur, into what will be a viable creature of business evolution.[1]

---

[1]Speech before the Issues Management Association, New York, 1983.

Adopting a two-pronged approach, the company used its strategic planning staff to develop diversification efforts away from growth industries toward growth opportunities in mature ones, including the insurance industry. At the same time, the issues management focus was on strengthening the company's basic business, steel and manufacturing, in the face of technological, social, regulatory, and competitive changes.

In pursuing the second task, American Can adopted a four-step issues management system described as the identification of major issues facing the company's basic business, an analysis of their probable impact on the future of the company, strategy development for their successful resolution, and action program implementation to carry out those strategies.

The major health issue facing the industry concerned the presence of lead in food cans. Lead had been present in food cans since 1908, when the soldering of can seams entered the manufacturing process. Until the 1970s, there was only one way to make such cans. The metal was bent into a cylinder, the seam soldered, and the ends capped. The process exposed consumers to minute quantities of lead, no greater than those present in the air the customers breathed in their homes. However, as the Food and Drug Administration's analytical methods and tools grew more refined, even the small amounts of lead involved began to loom larger as a public health issue.

As the new research emerged, American Can voluntarily redesigned its manufacturing process to reduce the amount of lead present, *before* the FDA mandated reductions. Thus, when the mandate came and the rest of the industry was forced to comply, American Can was in a superior competitive position, capable of meeting its customers' immediate needs.

However, further analysis of the lead issue convinced the company's senior management that the issue would never go away as long as *any* lead was present in the cans. Management believed that on the basis of current research any amount of lead in food cans was technologically unnecessary. This became the company's issue strategy. It spent nearly $80 million to convert its manufacturing processes from soldered to welded food cans or two-piece seamless ones of its own invention.

Connor believes this strategy will pay off handsomely both in economic and social terms, as lead continues to disappear from the food stream in this country. Thus, by facing the issue, the company discovered that it could totally resolve the issue by a unilateral act, which will have long-term benefits in advancing the company's competitive position and its public acceptance.

PNM—A REGIONAL APPLICATION

In addition to the many national and multinational corporations using the issues management approach, a number of regional companies have been successful with it also.

One noteworthy example is the Public Service Company of New Mexico, or PNM, as it is known in that state. It has developed one of the more effective issues management systems, supported by sophisticated research, monitoring, and planning techniques.

As in all successful integrations of issues management in a corporation, the CEO was personally involved in its creation. PNM's CEO Jerry D. Geist not only decided his company needed the system, he helped design it and personally oversees its operations. To do this, he went outside for an experienced management consulting/public affairs firm and an experienced public official to come aboard as PNM's staff director.

Together with Ashton B. Collins, Jr., president of Reddy Communications, Inc., and Albuquerque's former mayor, David Rusk, Geist designed his company's system. His decision to embrace the new management technique was prompted by a legislative firestorm he found himself in.

PNM, an electric utility, is New Mexico's largest domestic corporation, with over $2.7 billion in assets. It had begun to diversify into coal mining, land development, water systems, manufacturing, venture capital, and other businesses. In February 1982, the state legislature banned PNM's new rate-making process, based on a cost of servicing index. It also nearly permanently banned utility diversification, settling instead on a 15-month moratorium. By May that year, Geist had his new issues management system installed.

The system's top issue policy body is the Corporate Management Committee, composed of senior officers. The Issues Analysis Section under Director Rusk organizes the committee's agenda, prepares staff reports, and follows through to facilitate committee decisions. The section is responsible for issue identification in the areas of rates and regulatory process; diversification/competition; power supply/capacity; size, credibility, and reputation; and various other issues affecting subsidiaries.

The company uses interdepartmental task forces for each issue. The task forces make issue impact assessments, analyze policy options, and recommend company positions. They develop a communications matrix for each issue, listing target audiences, frame of reference, desired outcome, company message, and media delivery systems.

Every Monday morning, the Corporate Management Committee reviews a "weekly issues matrix" with Rusk. The issues matrix is a computerized report targeting 15 or more key activities and issues. It is backed up by a network of updated project reports, using the same computerized system with input from key line managers. This system enables the Issues Analysis Section to monitor several hundred company activities and bring the important issue-related ones to top management's attention.

Using this system, PNM responded to the public opposition to its diversification plans in the following manner. Its analysis revealed that small businesses and legislators viewed PNM as a giant octopus about to take over the state through its unexplained diversification efforts.

Research also revealed that New Mexicans placed the highest priority on the need for more industry and jobs in the state. The public's desire was compatible with PNM's diversification goal, to bring new businesses and enterprises with their jobs to the state, where PNM supplied half of the population's electrical energy needs.

PNM decided to offset the fears regarding its diversification activities by communicating its diversification program's goal: economic development in the state. Its basic message "Building a Stronger New Mexico."

The campaign was launched in July 1982. The company identified more than 1,000 opinion leaders, employees, and shareholders who agreed to contact their legislators to support PNM's economic development plans. Company representatives spoke to more than 200 organizations in the state, appeared on a dozen public affairs programs, and secured organizational and editorial endorsements.

The campaign had built up a large constituency by the time the state legislature next met. In March 1983 the state senate rejected the bill that would permanently ban utility diversification, with some proponents of the original bill leading the fight on the senate floor to defeat it.

Since then, PNM's issues management philosophy has resulted in the company's joining with some of its consumer critics to help resolve other public policy issues in New Mexico.

INTERNATIONAL ISSUES

Although issues management as a conscious technique began in American corporations primarily because of domestic issues, it evolved into an international issues management system in several multinational corporations. The earliest and most professional system was developed by Monsanto Company, an early adopter of the issues management technique.

Under the leadership of Margaret A. Stroup, Monsanto's director of strategic issues analysis, the company's domestic issues management system was expanded to its European, Latin American, and Asian/Pacific operations. Separate issues identification committees made up of corporate executives in those areas were established. These committees deal directly with the issues affecting them and once a year report new and ongoing issues analyses and results to Monsanto's Corporate Emerging Issues Committee in St. Louis. Stroup, one of the outstanding corporate issues management executives, reports that once the issues management concept is grasped by executives in other countries, the results are always positive. Globalwide attention is given issues that will impact Monsanto in the 1990s. Monsanto's goal is to integrate responses to identified issues into all management systems within the organization.

The most complex issues management case resolved in recent years was the long-running one Nestlé faced.

THE NESTLÉ BOYCOTT

In contrast to the Hooker Chemicals disaster, the Nestlé infant formula case is a classic of "before and after" the application of issues management. Blowing aside the smoke that has come from our national media, the record reveals this sequence of events.

Like most cyclones, the issue began as a cloud no bigger than a man's hand—in fact, one man's hand. In 1969 at a United Nations-sponsored meeting in Bogatá, Colombia, Dr. Derrick B. Jelliffe, then the director of the Caribbean Food and Nutrition Institute, charged that the infant food industry's marketing practices were the major factor contributing to the decline of breast feeding in the Third World. He further charged that an increase in the use of infant food products, given the poor hygenic conditions found in these countries, contributed to infant disease, malnutrition, and death.

Dr. Jelliffee followed up his charges with an article published in 1971, in which he coined the phrase "commerciogenic malnutrition." Speaking in London in July 1973 at a CIBA Foundation symposium, he disparaged a U.N. group's effort to develop policy covering the matter and opined that "some other group may have to take a more aggressive, Nader-like stance" on the issue.

One appeared within a few week's time, announcing its presence in a magazine, the *New Internationalist*, published under the sponsorship of three United Kingdom-based charitable organizations, Oxfam, Christian Aid, and Third World First. In an article entitled "The Baby Food Tragedy," Nestlé among all the infant formula makers was singled out for particular attention and excoriation. Two months later, the magazine followed with an editorial, "Milk and Murder." The editorial announced its rejection of Nestlé's offer for the editors to come to its headquarters and review its scientific and marketing data. More important, the magazine didn't publish Nestlé's written refutation of many of the charges, which the editors had solicited *after* publication of the original article.

Although the magazine disdained Nestlé's offer, Mike Muller, a freelance journalist on assignment for another British charity, War on Want, appeared at Nestlé's Swiss headquarters later that year. Muller professed concern about the *New Internationalist* report. Nestlé's management spent two days answering his questions. Early in 1974 his report was published by War on Want, complete with a London press conference. The report was entitled: *The Baby Killer.*

In June 1974, Muller's booklet was translated into German and published in Switzerland under the title *Nestlé Kills Babies* by the Third World Working Group, a Swiss organization with but 17 members, mostly university students.

Confident that it could show that the booklet's accusations had no foundation, Nestlé immediately filed a libel suit against the publisher and translators. However, Nestlé had not taken into account the ultraslowness of the Swiss judicial system—18 months passed before the first hearings were scheduled and 6 more before the decision. Although the decision came down in Nestlé's favor, with a finding that the publishers were guilty of libel and the assessment of a fine, Nestlé had not anticipated that the lawsuit would give the activists media credibility. The media attention not only brought financial support to the critics, it energized a transatlantic migration of the issue to the United States.

Following the publication of *The Baby Killer*, two major attacks on Nestlé were mounted in the United States. Consumers Union published its report, *Hungry for Profits* in 1975, unusual in itself for C.U. generally confined its reports to American consumer products and services. The same year a German-produced film shot in Kenya, "Bottle Babies," was distributed through the efforts of the Infant Formula Action Coalition (INFACT), an organization supported by the full spectrum of U.S. activists from the clergy, consumer organizations, labor unions, and teachers' associations. INFACT's objectives included "educating the U.S. public about the role of Nestlé and developing strategies along with their European counterparts to pressure that giant," according to a leader of the American-based Interfaith Center on Corporate Responsibility, which was sponsored by various religious orders and the National Council of Churches.

In July 1977, INFACT launched a boycott of Nestlé products sold in the United States, even though Nestlé's American companies neither produced nor sold infant formula for domestic consumption or export.

In 1978, the activists' cause was taken up by Senator Edward M. Kennedy, who decided to hold hearings on the infant formula issue. Nestlé was invited to testify. It decided to appear, even though it was a Swiss-based company that manufactured and marketed infant formula outside the territorial authority of the U.S. government.

As it prepared for the hearings, Nestlé's management became convinced that the activists' attack on the infant formula marketing issue was merely one manifestation of a worldwide attack on capitalism. It decided to prepare a collection of statements by its critics that would demonstrate their apparent political orientation. Included in the statements gathered were those made by an INFACT coordinator at a 1978 symposium organized by Clergy and Laity Concerned: "It's not just babies, it's not just multinational corporations, it's class conflict and class struggle.... I think ultimately what we're trying to do is take an issue-specific focus campaign and move in conjunction with other issue-specific campaigns into a larger, very wide, very class-conscious campaign and reassert our power in this country, our power in this world."

For the Kennedy hearings, Nestlé brought in Dr. Oswaldo Ballarin, chairman of its operations in Brazil, one of the largest infant formula markets in the Third World. At the hearings, Dr. Ballarin made the incredible allegation, at least to American ears, that the attack on the infant formula industry was being led by "a worldwide church organization with the stated purpose of undermining the free enterprise system." A bemused Senator Kennedy asked Dr. Ballarin to identify the members of the conspiracy. He was told they included the World Council of Churches and the National Council of Churches! Dr. Ballarin later apologized for his statements.

This event proved to be the low point in Nestlé's effort to resolve the infant formula issue, for following the hearings in 1978 the National Council of Churches' delegates voted 280 to 2 at their annual conferences to support INFACT's year-old boycott of Nestlé products.

Although Senator Kennedy did not draft legislation as a result of the hearings, at the request of the formula manufacturers he did contact the World Health Organization's director-general to ask for a conference to establish an international marketing code. WHO agreed to set the conference for 1979.

The 1979 WHO conference resulted in a consensus document, which was expanded and refined over the next two years. In May

1981 the Code of Marketing for Infant Formula was adopted by the WHO assembly, 118 to 1. Ironically enough, the country in which Nestlé's critics were most active, the United States, voted against the code because of constitutional conflicts.

The activists' attack on Nestlé from 1973 on was a classic textbook campaign that could have been forecast by anyone who had spent a few hours reading Saul Alinsky's two books, *Reveille for Radicals* (University of Chicago Press, 1945) and *Rules for Radicals* (Random House, 1971). These two books have served as primers for activists in Western democracies, including the Catholic and Protestant clergies, for several decades. Experienced public affairs and issues managers have known since 1972 that these books not only coach citizen activists in strategy and tactics, but also provide examples of the probable and expected corporate responses to the tactics.

Nestlé's reactions were also predictable conventional public relations crisis responses—until 1981. After hiring and dismissing two of the largest public relations firms in this country, Nestlé finally turned to a veteran American issues manager, Rafael D. Págan, Jr. Págan had worked as an issues manager for two large multinational corporations, the International Nickel Company and Castle & Cooke, Inc.

He has given this account of the agreement he struck with senior management in Nestlé's Swiss headquarters:

> First, we would deal with the issue—not the activist critics. Nestlé wasted too much time trying to persuade, with scientific facts, hard-core activists whose motives were clouded by anti-business biases. Second, we would receive full support and authority from the highest levels of corporate management. Third, some dramatic measures were required in our relations with various publics. Changes in policy would be required and the continued maintenance of the highest standard of corporate ethics was critical. Fourth, management at all levels would be involved as active participants in the strategy—this would be a total corporate effort in which all functions would play a role in an integrated strategy. Fifth, the development of a strategy and the conduct of operations in that strategy would be handled by a Nestlé group—a new company specially tailored with expertise in food, science, and nutrition as well as in the political and sociological disciplines. This group was to be based in Washington, D.C.[2]

---

[2]R. D. Págan, Jr., speech before the Issues Management Association, New York, 1983.

Págan discovered that even though Nestlé's infant formula sales account for almost half of the market worldwide, they are but 2.5 percent of its total business. Nevertheless, Nestlé's management was totally committed to the marketing of infant formula because internally it was an emotional issue. The company had been founded in 1869 by Henri Nestlé for the purpose of marketing his invention of infant formula.

Management was morally outraged by the charges that its marketing efforts did not also encourage breast feeding. The company believed it had always followed that policy since Mr. Nestlé's first guidebook to new mothers was published in 1871. It stated: "During the first months, the mother's milk will always be the most natural nutriment, and every mother able to do so should herself suckle her children." Thus, management realized that the issue had to be managed internally as well as externally.

Next, corporate staff reanalyzed the basic issue, which helped management understand that it was political as well as nutritional. Then it analyzed the opposition, diagnosing their objectives and motivations. The articulated objective of all the organizations in opposition was to have Nestlé reform its formula marketing practices in the Third World. Págan and his associates then searched for "inarticulated objectives" of the opposition organizations.

Nestlé decided to work with those organizations whose articulated and inarticulated objectives were the same, for example, the religious groups and "critics of conscience." They decided there was no point in working with organizations whose stated objectives were determined to be "only a cover for conflicts and goals distinctly different from the issue of health."[3] However, outrageous charges by such organizations would be quickly and publicly challenged.

With this policy clearly in mind, Nestlé created the Nestlé Coordination Center for Nutrition, Inc., in Washington, D.C., and appointed Págan president.

Págan's strategy was as follows:

> We had to regain, or in some cases establish, credibility with those organizations (critics of conscience) so they would believe us when we said we were committed to doing what was right, and we had to establish

---

[3]Ibid.

a clear-cut standard of what was right. We found this clear-cut, internationally accepted standard in the WHO Code. We had to regain the initiative from the critics so we could control the direction of the issue, and we had to leave in place an unimpeachable base of objective evaluation of our actions in order to fend off the organizations with inarticulated objectives and motivation.[4]

Under this strategy, Nestlé endorsed the WHO Code of Marketing for Breastmilk Substitutes the day it was passed in May 1981. Shortly thereafter, Nestlé representatives testified in support of the code before Congress. This allowed the company to express for the record its commitment to the code in an atmosphere of "legitimacy and official review," in contrast to its unhappy appearance at the Kennedy hearings.

Next, the company approached the United Methodist Task Force on Infant Formula, whose members had individually endorsed the boycott, to discuss specific implementation of the WHO code. After 18 months of discussion, Nestlé adopted specific instructions for implementing the code worldwide. In 1982, it appointed an independent commission of scientists, clergy, and ethicists to audit the company's compliance with the code. The audit commission, chaired by former Secretary of State Edmund S. Muskie, issued its first quarterly report in September 1982.

The following month the Methodists' General Council of Ministries, on the advice of its task force, voted not to join the boycott. Other churches soon reached the same conclusion. The American Federation of Teachers voted to withdraw from the boycott, as did various other organizations. The *Washington Post*, Nestlé's severest media critic, called for a stop in the rhetorical attacks. Finally, on January 24, 1984, the International Nestlé Boycott Committee announced suspension of the boycott of Nestlé products. Two days later, INFACT announced the end of its boycott.

At the Washington press conference announcing the Nestlé boycott suspension, INFACT Chairman Douglas A. Johnson addressed his closing remarks to Nestlé's competitors: "Nestlé's leadership must also be followed by other companies, especially those of the U.S. These companies have relished sitting in the sidelines during the 6½-year Nestlé boycott, and the responsible

---

[4]Ibid.

FIGURE 12-1   Life Cycle of a Strategic Issue

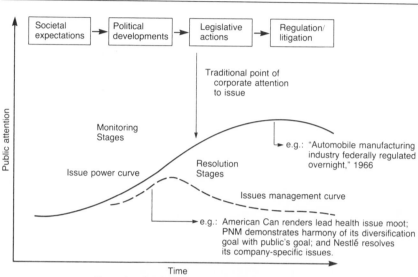

commitments won from Nestlé have been unfairly exploited to expand their market share. . . . Today, we are serving notice on these companies: now they move to center stage. Nestlé's competitors will be the focus of our attention at the upcoming International Strategy Conference in Mexico City."

Thus, the issue has left Nestlé, but its life cycle will encompass Nestlé's competitors before it moves into its quiescent stage, and another one takes its place.

Págan makes the following assessment of the issues manager: "Unless we can harmonize corporate goals with society's goals— or the public's goals—we have failed in our profession and in the most critical calling of the issues manager."[5]

---

[5]Ibid.

CHAPTER THIRTEEN

Is Issues Management for Your Company?

As the preceding case histories illustrate, the successful and widespread adoption of the issues management process rests on one simple fact. As a process driven by the concept of public policy foresight and action planning, it can be adapted to the management style, organizational structure, and resources of any company or organization. No one model, technique, or set of procedures need be rigidly followed.

The following questions and considerations are offered as a practical guide for executives wishing to determine whether they need or can confidently hope to use an issues management capability in their companies.

PUBLIC POLICY RELEVANCE

How relevant is the public policy process to your company? Are you in a regulated business? How relevant is your company to the public policy process? Is it vested with a public interest as are financial institutions, utilities, and similar companies? Is it unionized or targeted regularly by consumer advocates or politicians? Could the way you do business make your company or industry the object of legislative or regulatory interest in the future? Is the perceived social utility of your company's products or services questioned by organized constituencies?

If any of these questions are relevant, then your company would benefit from an issues management system.

INTERNAL VERSUS EXTERNAL STAFF

Does your trade association have an issues management system in place? (The American Society of Association Executives inaugurated in 1983 a special training course for association executives.)

If the answer is no, then the creation of a company issues management capability should be considered.

If your association has a system, is it sufficient for your company's needs? Additionally, is your company unique or a maverick within the industry?

If your company needs broader or more specific foresight and planning information, then an internal corporate system is in order. This is especially true if your company has needs different from other's in your industry or if your company considers itself a maverick and seeks its own solutions to industry problems. Likewise, companies seeking to assume a leadership role in their industry on public matters would want an additional capacity to deal with issues.

Smaller companies frequently have no need for an internal staff. They can assign experienced managers to their association's issues committee to make sure they are represented in industry decisions and collect issue information needed to keep their internal management informed.

SETTING UP AN INTERNAL CAPABILITY

Is senior management sufficiently aware of the need for and value of an internal issues management capability? Since all high-priority issues facing a company always require policy decisions at the top of a company before action can be taken to forestall or resolve them, an internal process is not cost effective if the staff's work is not for the use of senior management.

Departments in some large corporations (public affairs, public relations, planning, and personnel) have created their own systems for their team's use. However, experience has shown that the difficulty of trying to get their issues and policy recommendations on senior management's agenda frequently resulted in failure, frustration, and a sizable waste of staff time and the department's budget.

If an issues management engine is to be of value, it must be hooked up to the corporate drive shaft and connected to the operating wheels. This can occur only when senior management, meaning the CEO, makes a sincere commitment to the process and assigns responsibility for issues management to senior management, not to a department. Note that the case histories all involved either the CEO or the COO.

CORPORATE MISSION DRIVES THE PROCESS

Does your company have a written or well-understood corporate mission or set of goals? If so, the issues management process hangs from it, as does the strategic planning process. Any issue endangering the interests of your primary stakeholders endangers your company's viability. Therefore, it is an issue for your company. The mission statement and the stakeholders identified in it determine the issues your company can legitimately be concerned with. The mission statement defines your issues arena.

CAN YOUR COMPANY'S CULTURE ABSORB THE SYSTEM?

Is your company flexible enough to fit new techniques into management operations? The adoption of the issues management process by hundreds of companies over the past decade is proof of the fact that it can be fitted into almost any corporation. Only those corporations in which the CEO or COO is unwilling to share with subordinate managers consideration of corporate policy options is the system doomed. It should not be tried under such leaders.

But where top officers want to create a management system that elicits the most effective use of the talent, knowledge, and experience of upper and middle managers, the issues management system is effective. It has the added benefit of team-training the company's management pool in ways not otherwise possible.

STAFFING

Does your company have experienced public affairs (public relations or government relations) personnel knowledgeable in their profession and of issues management systems others are using? If not, issues management consultants are valuable in helping design a system and identify and train staff for you. (The membership list of the Issues Management Association includes most leading consultants, as well as corporate practitioners.)

BUDGETING

Is your company willing to allocate financial resources sufficient for staff to do the necessary scanning and monitoring of the issues of concern to your company? Information and foresight are as important a resource to management decisions as almost any other resource available to you. However, it costs money to develop.

PITFALLS AVOIDED AND TO BE AVOIDED

When issues management is top management's responsibility, territorial frictions as to the sharing of information and cooperation between departments are avoided. Cooperation between functional units is assured. This is because each unit's boss or boss's boss sits on the issues policy council.

Additionally, top management's assumption of responsibility overcomes problems created by the CEO's kitchen cabinet or "backstairs creepers" who slip into the CEO's office and quietly propose corporate policy that affects other department's operations without their knowledge. An issues management committee chartered by the CEO is not only healthy, it enhances management teamwork skills that carry into other areas.

The final pitfall to be avoided is to depend completely or too heavily on outside consultants, who place the final policy options and plans on the CEO's desk for his sole consideration. Consultants are invaluable, but only company employees are responsible for ongoing results, totally invested in the company's welfare—and susceptible to corrective discipline for policy failures.

There is also the matter of proprietary secrets and extrasensitive issues that cannot be discussed with outsiders until decisions are made on how to deal with them.

Perhaps the greatest benefit to a company is that a well-operating issues management system ensures the future life of the corporation by harmonizing corporate goals with society's goals.

General Robert E. Wood, one of the giants of American corporate management, seems to have anticipated the need for this system more than 40 years ago when he said: "Business must account for its stewardship not only on the balance sheet, but also in matters of social responsibility."

Issue management is designed to help corporations meet that responsibility, the new bottom line of public acceptance.

98TH CONGRESS
1st Session }

COMMITTEE PRINT

{ COMMITTEE
PRINT 98–B

FORESIGHT IN THE PRIVATE SECTOR: HOW CAN GOVERNMENT USE IT?

REPORT OF THE FORESIGHT TASK FORCE

PREPARED FOR THE USE OF THE

COMMITTEE ON ENERGY AND COMMERCE

U.S. HOUSE OF REPRESENTATIVES

January, 1983

130

MEMORANDUM OF TRANSMITTAL

U.S. House of Representatives,
Committee on Energy and Commerce,
Washington, D. C., March 14, 1983

TO: Members of the Committee

FROM: John D. Dingell, Chairman

I am pleased to transmit "Foresight in the Private Sector: How Can Government Use It?" to members of the Committee on Energy and Commerce.

This print is the report of a special task force on foresight initiated and coordinated by issues managers from several large corporations and one of this nation's major charitable organizations. In taking this initiative, the issues managers created a unique cooperative effort between themselves, this Committee, the Administration and a consultant to the Supreme Court. The Committee is printing the report of the task force as part of its ongoing effort to help Federal decision-makers anticipate future events.

This print is best viewed as a briefing book on the newly emerging field of issues management. Issues management is the practice of evaluating the social, political and environmental context in which an organization exists and attempting to position that organization to make maximum use of available opportunities to further its legitimate goals. The field is relatively young and it is only over the past several years that a body of techniques have emerged for accomplishing effective issues management. This print provides an overview of the new field and its current techniques in a format that should communicate effectively to governmental decision-makers.

The Committee is deeply indebted to all the individuals who participated on the task force and have made this report available for Committee use. The Committee is particularly indebted to Lynne Hall and Shell Canada for hosting the task force meetings and providing logistical support.

131

CONTENTS

■ Introduction

■ Strategic Vision
■ Strategic Process
  — Environmental Assessment
  — Organizational Assessment
  — Direction Setting
  — Implementation
  — Evaluation
■ Issues Management
■ Networking

■ Summary

■ Appendices

INTRODUCTION

This report represents the work of the Foresight Task Force assembled to assist in reviewing mechanisms for shaping long term policy with a view toward determining whether they could be made more effective through the utilization of planning, forecasting and analysis techniques currently used in the private sector.[*]

The objective in creating the Foresight Task Force, and more specifically, its parent organization — the May 20-21 Invitational Workshop[**], is that it might contribute to or even constitute the basis of a collaborative public/private sector effort resulting in more informed governance.

The specific purpose of the Foresight Task Force is to develop a catalog of potential capabilities drawn from private sector experience useful to the Legislative, Executive and as appropriate, the Judicial, branches of the United States Government.

[*]See "The Strategic Future: Anticipating Tomorrow's Crises; A Report Prepared for the Use of the Committee on Energy and Commerce", U.S. House of Representatives; Washington, D.C.: Government Printing Office, August 1981.

[**]See "Public Issue Early Warning Systems: Legislative and Institutional Alternatives," U.S. House of Representatives; Washington, D.C.: Government Printing Office, 1982.

The Foresight Task Force first met July 14-15 to review the context within which the governmental system operates and to determine, within that context, which of the various private sector capabilities seems most appropriate. The Task Force held additional meetings on October 29 and December, 1982.

What shaped much of the Task Force's deliberations was the assumption that governmental entities, like private sector entities, increasingly reside in a strategic environment where critical choices must be made concerning the allocation of resources to define and accomplish specific objectives. This assumption accounts for the report's exceeding the originally specified foresight boundaries and placing foresight in the broader context of strategic activity.

The report begins with a summary of strategic vision, followed by a generic model of the strategic process. It then proceeds with a description of the process elements and concludes with thoughts concerning next steps in the program initiated by the House Committee on Energy and Commerce in 1981. Because this report is basically a resource document, only the barest outline of each topic is provided.

A glossary of terms used in this report is contained in Appendix A. A list of Foresight Task Force membership is contained in Appendix B. Full size illustrations of all graphic material contained in the report is available in a separate chart pack.

foresight task force

agenda

JULY 14-15, 1982
PRESIDENTIAL SUITE

WATERGATE HOTEL
WASHINGTON, D.C. 20037

JULY 14

■ Review of Task Force Purpose and Product   L. Hall
■ Briefing on Congressional Foresight Capacity   F. Potter
■ Briefing on White House Foresight Capacity   R. Bledsoe
■ Briefing on Library of Congress Foresight Capacity   D. Little
■ Task Force Reviews Guidelines and Expectations of Briefings   Task Force

JULY 15

■ Task Force Members Review Applicable Models, Approaches, etc.   Task Force
■ Task Force Selects Elements Useful for Incorporation into Draft   Task Force
  Catalog Package

STRATEGIC VISION

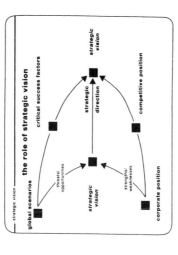

the role of strategic vision

When faced with meeting the challenge of the strategic future referred to in the August, 1981 report of the House Committee on Energy and Commerce, the private sector typically relies on its strategic management capacities guided by a central strategic vision.

Strategic vision is an explicit, shared understanding of the nature and purpose of the organization. It specifies what the organization is and should be (rather than what it does). As such, it serves as the organization's blueprint for success.

Strategic vision motivates and guides the organization in minimizing the impact of threats and maximizing the benefits of opportunities posed by the external environment. Strategic vision stabilizes the organization in times of turbulence and uncertainty.

In the view of the Task Force, an eloquent statement of national strategic vision was set forth in the Declaration of Independence.

STRATEGIC PROCESS

The strategic process* used in the private sector generally consists of six building blocks:

- Analysis of the External Environment.
- Analysis of the Internal Environment.
- Direction Setting.
- Definition and Selection of Base and Contingency Plans.
- Implementation.
- Performance Evaluation.

Given that the fundamental challenges are common to both sectors, the same model may be useful in the public sector.

The following summarizes the basic building blocks, while subsequent sections of the report go into greater depth in each area.

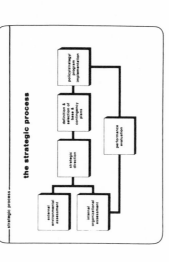

the strategic process

*As used in this context, strategic refers to anticipating change and making choices among options which favor the organization's adaptive capacities.

Analysis of the External Environment: Identification of Threats and Opportunities

This is the principal area traditionally associated with foresight. It involves judgment concerning alternative outcomes of existing trends as well as speculation about emerging developments. Specifically, it focusses on threats and opportunities.

Analysis of the Internal Environment: Identification of Strengths and Weaknesses

This involves self-assessment in which the organization evaluates its human, financial, technological and structural/informational capacities and potentialities. Specifically, it focuses on the organization's strengths and weaknesses.

Direction Setting: Specification of Mission, Goals, Objectives

The strategic process is usually embedded within a vision which provides guidance for the organization. Direction setting renders this vision concrete in terms of defining an operational mission, goals and objectives.

4

137

Definition and Selection of Base and Contingent Plans

This part of the process involves identification of alternative courses of action under alternative future conditions.

Implementation

Usually, this activity involves accountability and execution.

Performance Evaluation

Performance evaluation compares actual with expected results and identifies the reasons for and magnitude of differences.

Constituent elements of the strategic process are summarized on pages 7-19.

6

ENVIRONMENTAL ASSESSMENT

Environmental assessment usually involves one or more of four activities:

- ■ Scenario Construction.
- ■ Premises Quantification.
- ■ Monitoring.
- ■ Scanning.

There is no rule that all four must be used, or used in the order specified.

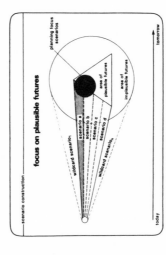

Scenario Construction

Scenarios are comprehensive, internally consistent narratives describing a variety of plausible futures. Usually, they are based on assumptions concerning complex interactions among international, regional, domestic and/or local social, economic, political and technological influences.

scenario construction

scenario development process

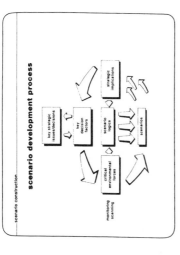

monitoring scanning

key strategic issues/decisions

key decision factors

scenario logics

critical environmental forces

strategic implications

scenarios

scenario construction

alternative scenarios

int'l political/ economic conditions	major political thrusts	
	centralization (country-building)	decentralization (region-building)
muddling along	scenario a	scenario b
restructured growth after crisis	scenario c	scenario d

Scenarios are useful because they provide an explicit and realistic frame of reference for the key forces/ uncertainties that may impinge on specific strategic issues and/or decisions. The objective of scenario construction is to develop a planning focus against which to evaluate strengths and weaknesses, make base and contingency plans and allocate resources.

The first step in scenario construction is the identification of key strategic issues and/or decisions. The next step is the identification and analysis of key variables affecting these issues and/or decisions. Typically, this leads to the specification of a variety of scenario logics encompassing the main driving forces critical to the outcome of the issues and/or decisions. These logics give the scenarios distinct thrusts and directions distinguishing each from the others, thus facilitating the formulation of specific, but flexible, base and contingency plans. The third and final step in the scenario construction process is the identification of strategic implications, i.e. the threats and opportunities implied by each scenario. This information, when combined with the results of self assessment (strengths and weaknesses), leads to the identificat on of leverage points where the organization's plans may be expected to be maximally effective in defining and accomplishing desired goals and objectives.

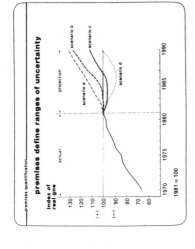

premises define ranges of uncertainty

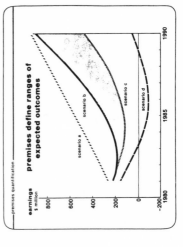

premises define ranges of expected outcomes

Premises Quantification

Once the scenarios' logics and main driving forces are identified, key variables (usually expressed as time series trends) can be projected for each scenario by use of tools and techniques, such as trend impact, cross impact, delphi, extrapolation, econometric modelling, etc.

An example of premises quantification and its relationship to scenario construction is shown in illustrations to the right. From among this company's four scenarios, two have been selected for base and contingency planning purposes (scenario b and c.) Key variables, i.e. factors of major strategic significance such as economic performance, as measured by gne, and corporate earnings, are then forecast according to the assumptions applicable in each of the two planning focus scenarios. The result is a bounded range of outcomes within which direction setting, policy and strategy formulation and resource allocation planning can take place.

9

142

Scanning/Monitoring

Environmental scanning may be best likened to a radar screen where random signals are registered which an observer then analyzes for possible pattern formation.

Environmental monitoring may best be likened to an electrocardiogram where the behavior of known variables is tracked or monitored for actual vs anticipated performance.

Two approaches to scanning and monitoring are widely used in the private sector. These are illustrated to the right. While these approaches represent the commercially available products of a particular consulting house, they are descriptive of the procedures generally undertaken by the private sector irrespective of whether that consulting house is involved.

10

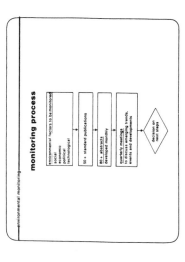

ORGANIZATIONAL ASSESSMENT

There are four separate, but related resource assessments a company typically carries out on itself. These evaluate the organization's strengths and weaknesses in the areas of:

- People.
- Money.
- Technology.
- Information.

Human Resource Assessment

This assessment usually involves a comparison of the skill base required by the strategic direction with that of the existing skill base. The purpose is to ensure that the necessary skill base is or will be in place to fulfill the organization's mission, goals and objectives. In addition to the inventory approach illustrated to the right other approaches involve perception testing of key constituencies which may include such procedures as opinion polls, personal and/or group interviews, surveys and/or group meetings.

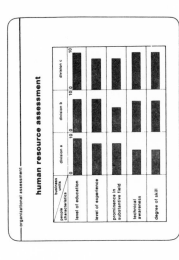

organizational assessment

human resource assessment

people characteristics \ business units	division a		division b		division c	
	0	10	0	10	0	10
level of education						
level of experience						
prominence in substantive field						
technical awareness						
degree of skill						

Financial Assessment

Usually, this assessment involves a series of analyses based on the concept of contribution to corporate value. For application in the public sector, concepts of cost/benefit and cost/effectiveness may be more appropriate.

The illustration to the right shows one company's approach in integrating this series of analyses into a single package. Key elements include (clockwise from upper left):

■ the *corporate value matrix*, showing how growth and profitability combine to determine corporate value, thereby providing a measurement of capability and criterion for choosing among strategic options.

■ the *operating portfolio*, displaying the basic strategic position of the business that determines its profitability potential.

■ the *strategy direction chart*, illustrating the resulting position of selected strategic options.

■ the *financial portfolio*, illustrating levels of expected profitability associated with a business' position in the operating portfolio and its strategic thrust indicated on the strategy direction chart.

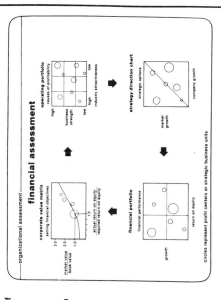

organizational assessment

financial assessment

corporate value matrix
setting financial objectives

3.0
2.0
1.0

market value
book value

1.0

actual return on equity
required return on equity

operating portfolio
causes of profitability

high

business
strength

low

high   low
industry attractiveness

strategy direction chart
strategic options

market
growth

company growth

financial portfolio
financial performance

growth

return on equity

circles represent profit centers or strategic business units

12

145

Technology Evaluation

Generally, this assessment, similiar to the human resources assessment, involves an inventory of the organization's existing technology compared with the technology necessary to fulfill the organization's mission, goals and objectives.

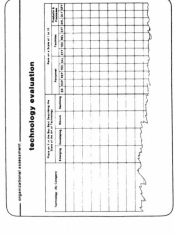

organizational assessment

technology evaluation

organizational assessment

technology evaluation continued

Information/Structural Assessment

There are few norms governing this area of self-assessment except that the guiding principle usually has to do with the efficient and effective flow of information for decision-making/strategy implementation purposes. In the private sector, the strategic business unit (sbu, sometimes referred to as a profit center) is usually the organizing principle for this analysis. In the public sector, the concept of accountability center may be a useful substitute.

14

DIRECTION SETTING

Setting strategic direction typically involves three steps. It is absolutely critical, however, that the organization's senior management participate in and actively lead this three step process. These steps include:

- Surveying present and prospective realities and potentialities.

- Identifying and testing alternative directions and profiles including their organizational and operational implications.

- Deciding on the direction and profile of the organization, periodically reviewing its legitimacy/viability and communicating these in the form of mission, goals and objectives to key stakeholder groups.

Missions, Goals/Objectives

What is meant by mission, goals and objectives is summarized as follows:

- *Mission*: What the organization is in business to accomplish, e.g. an energy company may be in business of discovering and developing energy resources for the purpose of producing and selling them at a profit.

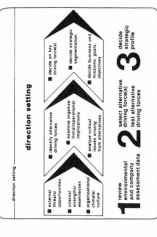

direction setting

external threats/opportunities
internal strengths/weaknesses
organizational climate/culture

1 review environmental and company assessment data

identify alternative driving forces
examine organizational/operational implications
analyze critical issues arising from alternatives

2 select alternative driving force(s)
test alternative driving forces

decide on key driving force(s)
decide strategic segmentation
decide business unit missions, goals, objectives

3 decide strategic profile

■ **Goals:** How the organization will carry out its mission, e.g. in the energy example, by pushing the exploration and development business, by maintaining profitable synergistic businesses and by divesting all other businesses.

■ **Objectives:** The specific measures of accomplishment specifying at which levels goals have been met, e.g. key projects must meet an 18-24% financial screening rate.

The product of the three step direction setting process includes:

■ A simple, concise statement of strategic direction adequate to guide both long term decision-making and short term day-to-day operations.

■ A commitment to that direction based on shared understanding throughout the organization and its major stakeholder groups.

■ A basis for policy, plans and program formulation and resource allocation.

■ A basis for identifying and handling critical strategic issues.

16

IMPLEMENTATION

The transition from mission, goals and objectives to implementation is frequently facilitated by use of a tree diagram. The illustration to the right, drawn from a recent publication aimed at state and municipal governments, shows only the main branches. Typically, these diagrams are extended to include specific tasks as well as accountabilities and performance measures.

implementation

Illustrative example: strategy diagram

objective	strategies	programs
revitalize downtown	encourage private rehabilitation of older structures	encourage investor response to federal tax credits
		provide industrial revenue bonds
		reduce development control risks
		raise demand for quality space
	improve infrastructure and maintenance	allow sale-leaseback of public facilities
		provide efficient fire protection
		improve assessments and user charges
		contract for mechanized trash removal
	improve traffic movement and parking	improve parking management system
		give tax and density credits for private parking development
		seek investment in new transportation forms
	control street crime	create juvenile jobs in architectural rehabilitation
		target tax incentives
		increase foot patrol
		motivate united way project

Generally, programs are implemented as follows:

- Assignment of accountability for accomplishment is made to a particular individual, team and/or department.

- Milestones of accomplishment and expected results are stated in explicit and measureable terms.

- Provision for periodic evaluation is made.

- As with every step in the strategic process, top management signals and periodically reinforces its commitment to the process.

18

EVALUATION

At a minimum, evaluation in the private sector typically involves:

■ A review of the extent to which strategies and programs have been implemented.
■ A review of actual vs expected results against prespecified goals and objectives.

Generally, three kinds of questions are asked:

■ Did the strategies and programs accomplish the desired goals and objectives within target ranges? If not, what adjustments may be necessary?
■ Are other adjustments required with respect to internal strengths and weaknesses?
■ Are other adjustments required with respect to changing external threats and/or opportunities?

Typically, in the private sector, evaluation and feedback serve as part of the management control system.

ISSUES MANAGEMENT

Issues management is interrelated with and contributes to the strategic process in the private sector. In its foresight dimension, it provides crucial intelligence concerning social, economic, political and technological trends, events and developments affecting the organization's strategic viability. It also establishes an agenda for and a means of marshalling participation in the public policy process when issues relate to that arena.

Specifically, the focus of issues management is strategic issues, i.e. those trends, events and developments which meet three criteria:

■ They could impact the organization's performance.

■ The organization must systematically marshall its collective resources to deal with them.

■ The organization may reasonably expect to exert some influence over their outcome.

—issues management

key questions

■ what is the probability that a given trend, event or development will become a *major* issue?

■ how great will the eventual impact on the institution be?

■ how likely is the impact to be focussed on the institution rather than diffused over the entire community?

■ when is the issue likely to peak
  — near-term?
  — medium-term?
  — long-term?

■ who are the major players and what position(s) are they likely to adopt?

■ what can the organization do to deal with the issue?

The goal of issues management in the private sector is early warning/early response so that an issue's positive potential can be encouraged/enhanced and its negative potential can be discouraged/inhibited. The objective of issues management is to identify an issue in its early stages of development before options are narrowed and liabilities expanded. *The earlier an issue is identified and dealt with, the more successful the issues management process.*

The notion behind issues management is that issues, like products, industries and even whole societies, are subject to lifecycle principles moving through emerging, developing, maturing and declining stages. Or, as it was once put from the private sector perspective: "The societal concerns of yesterday become the political issues of today, the legislated requirements of tomorrow, and the litigated penalties of the day after."*

*Ian H. Wilson
formerly of The General Electric Company, currently with SRI.

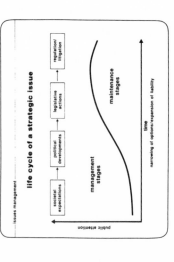

life cycle of a strategic issue

issues management

public attention

| societal expectations | → | political developments | → | legislative actions | → | regulation/ litigation |

management stages

maintenance stages

time
narrowing of options/expansion of liability

22

Four Stages of a Strategic Issue's Life Cycle

Within the four stages of an issue's life cycle critical developments occur.

■ *The Societal Expectations stage* signals structural changes, and gives rise to recognition, and often the politicization of an issue.

■ *The Political Developments stage* gives rise to the creation of ad hoc and/or formal organizations to deal with the issue.

■ *The Legislative Actions stage* signals a peak in public attention wherein the issue is defined in operational or legal terms and solutions, frequently in the form of laws and regulations are implemented.

■ *The Regulation/Litigation stage* represents a plateau in public attention when enforcement procedures become routine and penalties apply to those who ignore or violate the spirit, letter and/or intent of the law.

Sufficient foresight in the management stages can lead to organizational actions that may prevent advancement of an issue to the maintenance stages and that, in turn, may disclose positive opportunities for the organization.

issues management

Issues priority matrix

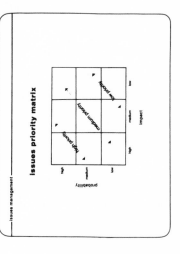

issues management

Issues management process
an illustrative example*

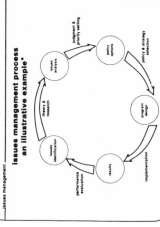

*Copyright, W. Howard Chase and Barrie L. Jones, 1977 revised.

The first step of a typical issues management process in the private sector is environmental and organizational analyses, covered in earlier sections of this report. The second step of the process involves a series of qualitative, sometimes quantitative, analyses evaluating the issues' probability of development, impact and timing. The third step of the process results in a display such as the one to the right where high probability/high impact, (thus, high priority issues) are located in the upper left hand portion of the matrix. In addition to analysis, the issues management process entails development of advocacies that marshall relevant expertise throughout the organization including senior management.

The functional (who does what with whom, when and where) aspects of issues management are perhaps best summarized by the experience of one company whose system is characterized by the double virtues of simplicity and effectiveness. This company's approach is based on a professional staff of issues managers closely linked to both operating units and senior management. Their activities are illustrated in the exhibit to the right.

NETWORKING

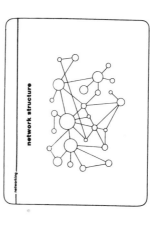

traditional organizational structure

network structure

When confronted with needs similar to those outlined by the House Committee on Energy and Commerce, the private sector typically employs a network model. (The Foresight Task Force itself is a network.)

A network is "a collection of individuals and/or organizations loosely and voluntarily linked with one another for a variety of mutually beneficial exchanges including ideas, information, resources and/or personnel."* Instead of depending on traditional, hierarchical forms of organization, a network depends on informal, interdependent structures which evolve over time and can easily ignore bureaucratic and institutional boundaries in executing their mission.

*See "The Basic Paradigm of Future, Socio-Cultural Systems", Virginia Hine, *World Issues*, April/May, 1977.

Formation of a network is generally based on three essential principles:

■ A common focus of interest among the membership.

■ Trust among the membership, promoting the free flow of ideas and information.

■ Protection of the sensitivity and possible confidentiality of the information exchanged.

The information exchanged ranges from raw data such as statistics and survey results to formal reports on particular topics or issues. The frequency of network meetings is anywhere from monthly to annually to once a lifetime depending upon the nature and purpose of the network. Typical periodicity in the private sector is from two to four times a year for networks concerned with foresight activities. However, some networks never meet but simply share information through telecommunications and/or other coordinating mechanisms.

With respect to foresight, there are a number of long-standing, private sector networks. Some of these are:

■ The Business Council, whose primary objective is to develop a constructive point of view on matters of public policy effecting the business interests of the country and to provide a medium for better understanding of government problems by the private sector.

■ The Council on Trends and Perspective of the U.S. Chamber of Commerce, whose purpose is to assist the Chamber and The Business Community to anticipate and think strategically about issues impacting business decision-making and operations, as well as to promote enlightened public discussion of long term issues vital to the interests of U.S. business.

- **The Business Round Table**, whose purpose is to anticipate and examine public policies and issues affecting the economy and the private sector and to develop and publicly espouse positions on these policies and issues.

- **Corporate Associates for Environmental Monitoring**, whose purpose is to provide a forum for the exchange of information concerning future social, economic, political and technological trends, events and developments affecting the private sector.

Finally, in this connection, a relevant model may be found in the voluntary sector, specifically from United Way of America, whose purpose is to assist 2,100 local, autonomous United Way organizations and agencies to anticipate and think strategically about issues affecting them, to provide tools, techniques and training, and to facilitate strategy development and implementation. To accomplish these goals, The United Way of America creates and maintains numerous networks linking government, corporate, academic, union, religious, etc., representatives.

—networking

characteristics of four networks committed to foresight activities

organization	when founded	type of membership	number of members	permanent staff
the business council	1933	business executives	200	3
the council on trends and perspective (u.s. chamber of commerce)	1966	academic and business upper management	34	1
the business round table	1972	corporate ceo's	194	20
corporate associates for environmental monitoring	1976	business representatives (upper and middle management)	20	none

SUMMARY

The Foresight Task Force has presented a catalog of potential capabilities, drawn from private sector experience. Government personnel may benefit from the use of concepts and techniques used by the private sector, both in their roles as strategic planners and as managers of government programs.

Individual members of the Task Force remain available to assist in interpreting and expanding upon this material.

Because of the dual constraints of time and space, it has not been possible to acknowledge the debt of gratitude that the Task Force owes to the many people and organizations who have contributed ideas and efforts to the foresight process discussed in this Report.

APPENDICES

- Appendix A   Glossary of Selected Terms

- Appendix B   Foresight Task Force Membership

- Appendix C   Foresight Task Force Chart Pack

appendix a

Glossary of Selected Terms

BASE PLANS — The base plan is the plan of action which is consistent with the most likely scenario and the organization's mission, goals, and objectives.

CONTINGENCY PLANS — The back up plan to the organization's base plan. The plan of action taken should the most likely or probable scenario develop in a pattern different than expected.

COST-BENEFIT — The relation between social and economic benefits and social and economic costs associated with the operation of the system under study including direct and indirect effects.

COST-EFFECTIVENESS — A term widely used in systems analysis and subsequently carried over into budget analysis. It signifies the relationship within an explicit and finite period (such as product life in service), of cost in dollars and other tangible values to effectiveness.

CROSS IMPACT ANALYSIS — An analytical technique for identifying the various impacts of specific events or well-defined policy actions on other events. It explores whether the occurrence of one event or implementation of one policy is likely to inhibit, enhance, or have no effect on the occurrence of another event.

DELPHI — An analytical technique using expert opinion and judgment. It consists of a carefully designed series of interrogations using written questionnaires, personal interviews and/or variations of computer conferencing, statistically evaluated information and opinion feedback, inhibiting the attribution of particular remarks to individual participants.

ECONOMETRIC MODELING — A form of modeling, usually done with computers which explores the components and interactions of a given economic system.

162

EXTERNAL ENVIRONMENT — All relevant elements or forces (social, economic, political, technological) external to and impacting on the organization.

INTERNAL ENVIRONMENT — All relevant elements or forces within an organization that impact on its components.

SCENARIOS — Narrative descriptions of alternative futures based on specific assumptions about relevant social, economic, political and technological forces and their interactions.

STRATEGIC BUSINESS UNIT — Within a corporation, an independently managed cluster or grouping of products with one or more markets that share similar competitive, growth and other risk and earnings potential characteristics.

STRATEGIC PROFILE — A set of characteristics describing the critical qualities of an enterprise within its field of industry (its opportunities, geographic and product line coverage, resources, costs competitive standing, special circumstances, etc.), and how those characteristics relate.

TREE DIAGRAM — An analytical tool sometimes referred to as a relevance tree. It is a diagrammatic technique for analyzing systems or processes in which distinct levels of complexity or hierarchy can be identified. It may be used to provide a hierarchical representation of the mission, goals, objectives and policies of a corporation.

TREND IMPACT ANALYSIS — An analytical technique for evaluating the potential effect of a set of chosen events upon a designated trend.

WILD CARD SCENARIO — A scenario with very low probability of occurrence, but high impact.

appendix b
Foresight Task Force Membership

Chairman:

Ms. Lynne Hall
General Manager
Corporate Strategy and
Business Development
Shell Canada Limited
505 University Avenue
Toronto, Ontario M5G 1X4
Canada

Task Force:

Mr. Roy R. Anderson
Vice President
Strategic Planning
Allstate Insurance Company
Northbrook, Illinois 60062

Dr. James C. Armstrong
Director, Corporate Policy Analysis
American Telephone and Telegraph Company
195 Broadway
New York, N.Y. 10007

Mr. Breck Arrington
Manager, Governmental Issues
Atlantic Richfield Company
515 S. Flower Street
Los Angeles, California 90071

Mr. William C. Ashley
Director, Issues Management
McDonald's Corporation
McDonald's Plaza
Oak Brook, Illinois 60521

Mr. Napier Collyns
Vice President
Scallop Corporation
One Rockefeller Plaza
New York, New York 10020

Mr. Raymond P. Ewing
President, Issues Management Association
c/o Allstate
Allstate Plaza
Northbrook, Illinois 60062

Mr. Hank Koehn
Vice President
Futures Research Division
Security Pacific National Bank
333 South Hope Street
Los Angeles, California 90071

Mr. Ralph L. Neubert
Management Consultant
7101 Bosque Boulevard
Waco, Texas 76710

Ms. Margaret A. Stroup
Director, Corporate Responsibility
Monsanto Company
800 N. Lindbergh Boulevard
St. Louis, Missouri 63167

Dr. George Wilkinson
Vice President
Strategic Planning
United Way of America
United Way Plaza
Alexandria, Virginia 22314

Resource
Participants: Mr. Jonathan P. Bellis
Office of Planning and Evaluation
Executive Office Building
1700 Pennsylvania Avenue, N.W.
Washington, D.C. 20500

Dr. Ralph Bledsoe
Special Assistant to
The President of the United States
Executive Office Building
Washington, D.C. 20500

Mr. Warren Citkins
Senior Staff Member
Advance Study Program
The Brookings Institution
1775 Massachusetts Ave. N.W.
Washington, D.C. 20036

Dr. John M. Clough, Jr.
Committee on Energy and Commerce
U.S. House of Representatives
Rayburn House Office Building
Washington, D.C. 20515

Mr. Walter A. Hahn
Visiting Professor of Public Affairs
George Washington University
Washington, D.C. 20052

Mr. Dennis Little
Specialist in Futures Research
and Population Policy
Congressional Research Service
Library of Congress
Washington, D.C. 20540

Mr. Frank M. Potter, Jr.
Chief Counsel and Staff Director
Committee on Energy and Commerce
U.S. House of Representatives
Rayburn House Office Building
Washington, D.C. 20515

165

appendix   c

FORESIGHT TASK FORCE

CHART PACK

January, 1983

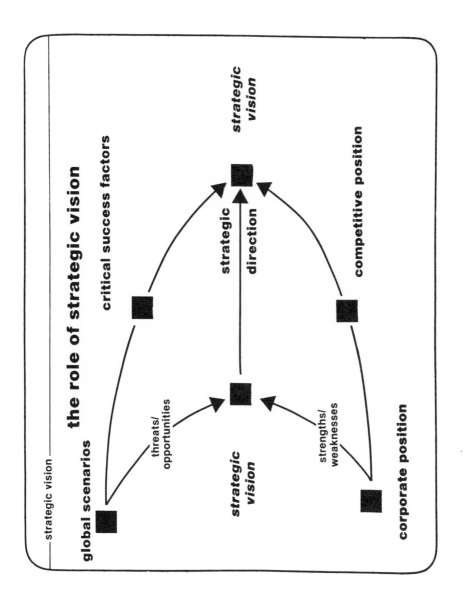

the role of strategic vision

strategic vision

critical success factors

strategic vision

global scenarios

threats/
opportunities

strategic
vision

strategic
direction

competitive position

strengths/
weaknesses

corporate position

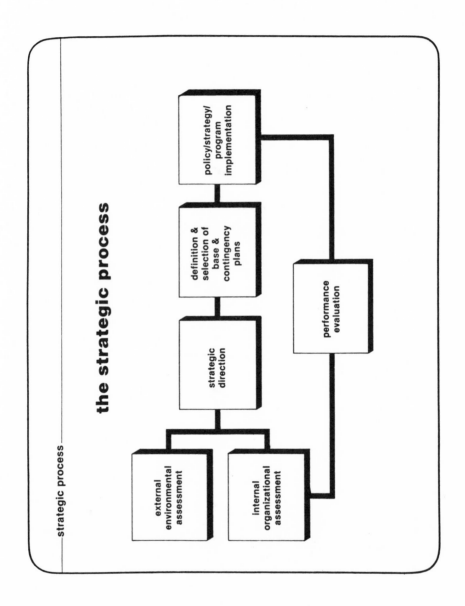

the strategic process

strategic process

policy/strategy/ program implementation

definition & selection of base & contingency plans

strategic direction

performance evaluation

external environmental assessment

internal organizational assessment

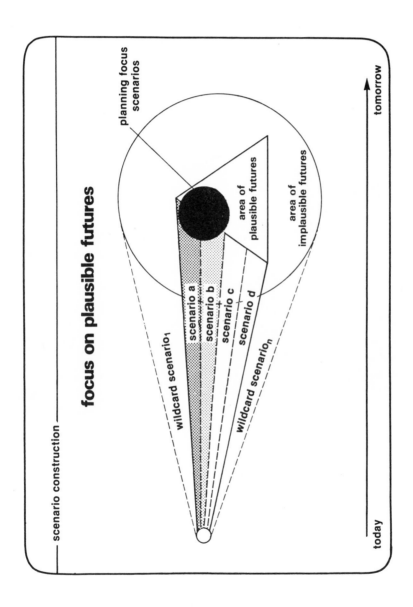

focus on plausible futures

scenario construction

today

tomorrow

planning focus scenarios

area of plausible futures

area of implausible futures

wildcard scenario₁

scenario a

scenario b

scenario c

scenario d

wildcard scenarioₙ

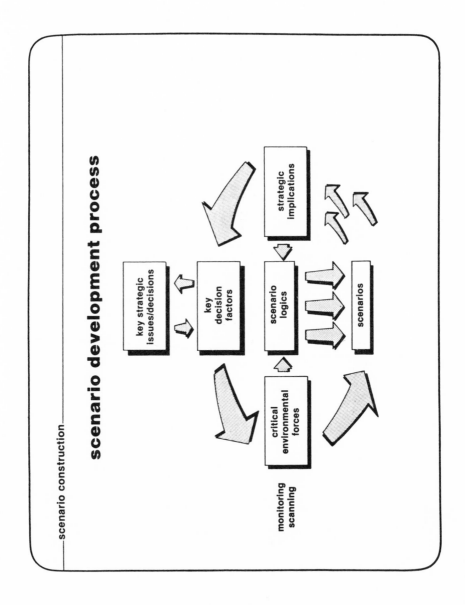

scenario construction

scenario development process

key strategic
issues/decisions

key
decision
factors

strategic
implications

scenario
logics

scenarios

critical
environmental
forces

monitoring
scanning

scenario construction

alternative scenarios

inter'l political/ economic conditions	major political thrusts	
	centralization (country-building)	decentralization (region-building)
muddling along	scenario a	scenario b
restructured growth after crisis	scenario c	scenario d

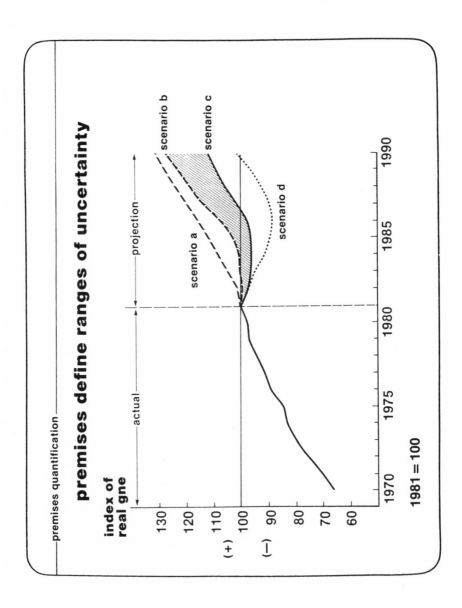

premises quantification

premises define ranges of uncertainty

1981 = 100

172

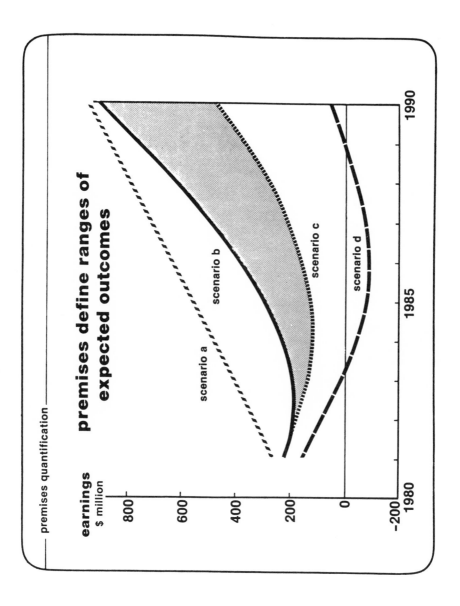

premises quantification

premises define ranges of expected outcomes

earnings
$ million

800
600
400
200
0
-200

1980   1985   1990

scenario a
scenario b
scenario c
scenario d

173

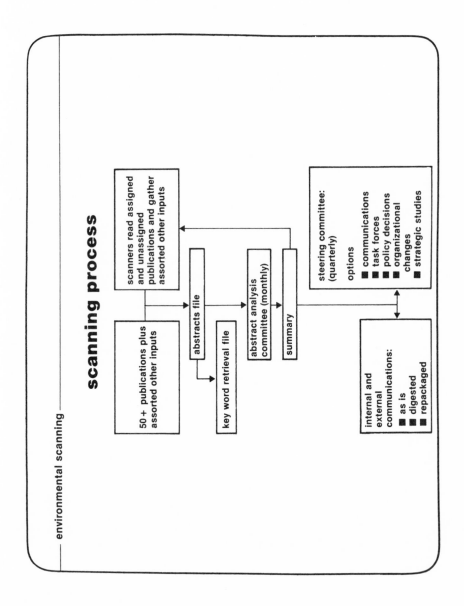

environmental scanning

scanning process

50 + publications plus assorted other inputs

scanners read assigned and unassigned publications and gather assorted other inputs

abstracts file

key word retrieval file

abstract analysis committee (monthly)

summary

steering committee: (quarterly)

options
- communications
- task forces
- policy decisions
- organizational changes
- strategic studies

internal and external communications:
- as is
- digested
- repackaged

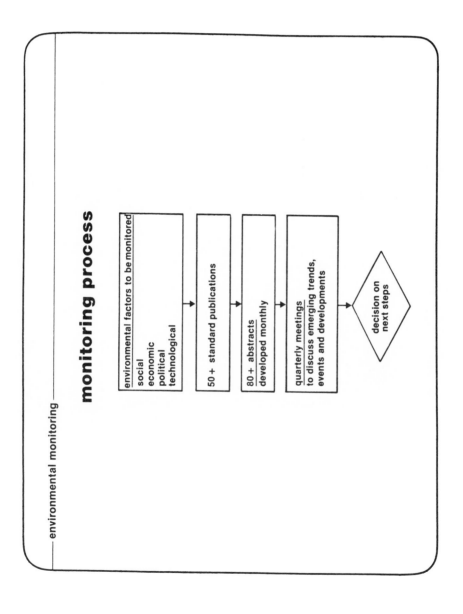

environmental monitoring

monitoring process

environmental factors to be monitored
social
economic
political
technological

50 + standard publications

80 + abstracts
developed monthly

quarterly meetings
to discuss emerging trends,
events and developments

decision on
next steps

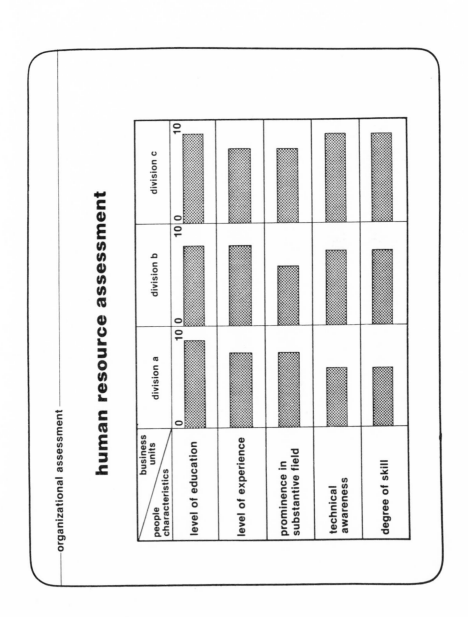

organizational assessment

human resource assessment

business units / people characteristics	division a		division b		division c	
	0	10	0	10	0	10
level of education						
level of experience						
prominence in substantive field						
technical awareness						
degree of skill						

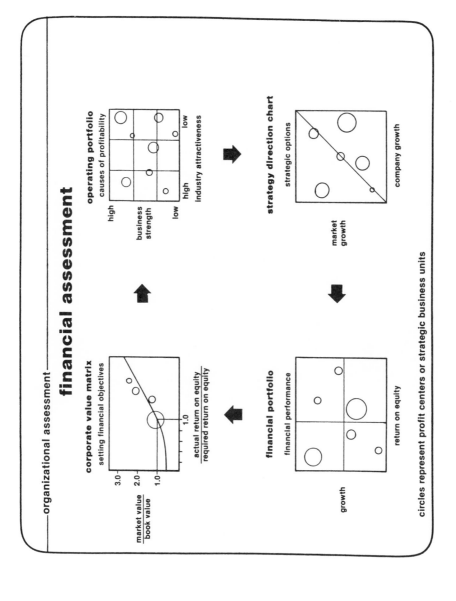

organizational assessment

financial assessment

corporate value matrix
setting financial objectives

market value
―――――――
book value

3.0
2.0
1.0

1.0

actual return on equity
―――――――――――――――
required return on equity

operating portfolio
causes of profitability

high

business
strength

low

high   low
industry attractiveness

strategy direction chart
strategic options

market
growth

company growth

financial portfolio
financial performance

growth

return on equity

circles represent profit centers or strategic business units

177

organizational assessment

technology evaluation

Technology (By Category)	Place an X in the Box Best Describing the State of the Art of Technology				Rank on a Scale of 1 to 10											
					Personnel				Facilities				Products & Processes		
	Emerging	Developing	Mature	Declining	ED	EXP	REP	TEC	SKL	EFF	TEC	REL	EXT	AVL	QLY	SFY

technology evaluation continued

Enter the Name(s) of Internal User(s) of this Technology	Place an X in the Box Best Identifying the Source of this Technology						Specify the Top Replacement/ Substitute/More Advanced Technology or Technologies	Specify the Owner/ Developer of the More Advanced Technology
	Developed Internally	Licenced or Contracted	USA	ECC	JAP	OTHER		

179

direction setting

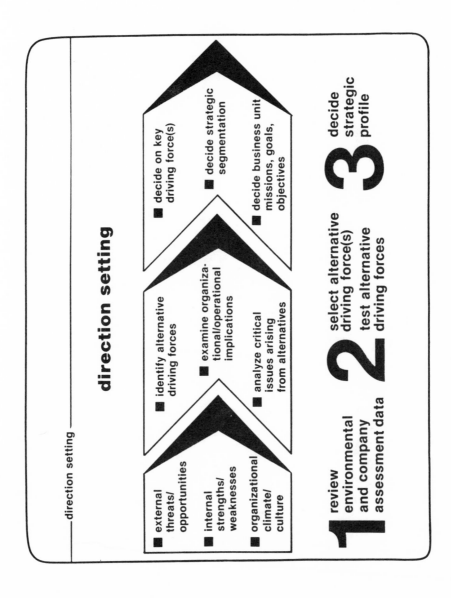

1 review
environmental
and company
assessment data

- external
  threats/
  opportunities
- internal
  strengths/
  weaknesses
- organizational
  climate/
  culture

2 select alternative
driving force(s)

2 test alternative
driving forces

- identify alternative
  driving forces
- examine organiza-
  tional/operational
  implications
- analyze critical
  issues arising
  from alternatives

3 decide
strategic
profile

- decide on key
  driving force(s)
- decide strategic
  segmentation
- decide business unit
  missions, goals,
  objectives

illustrative example: strategy diagram

objective	strategies	programs
revitalize downtown	encourage private rehabilitation of older structures	encourage investor response to federal tax credits
		provide industrial revenue bonds
		reduce development-control risks
		raise demand for quality space
	improve infrastructure and maintenance	allow sale-leaseback of public facilities
		provide efficient fire protection
		impose assessments and user charges
		contract for mechanized trash removal
	improve traffic movement and parking	improve parking management system
		give tax and density credits for private parking development
		seek investment in new transportation forms
	control street crime	create juvenile jobs in architectural rehabilitation
		target tax incentives
		increase foot patrol
		motivate united way project

181

key questions

■ what is the probability that a given trend, event or development will become a *major* issue?

■ how great will the eventual impact on the institution be?

■ how likely is the impact to be focussed on the institution rather than diffused over the entire community?

■ when is the issue likely to peak
  — near-term?
  — medium-term?
  — long-term?

■ who are the major players and what position(s) are they likely to adopt?

■ what can the organization do to deal with the issue?

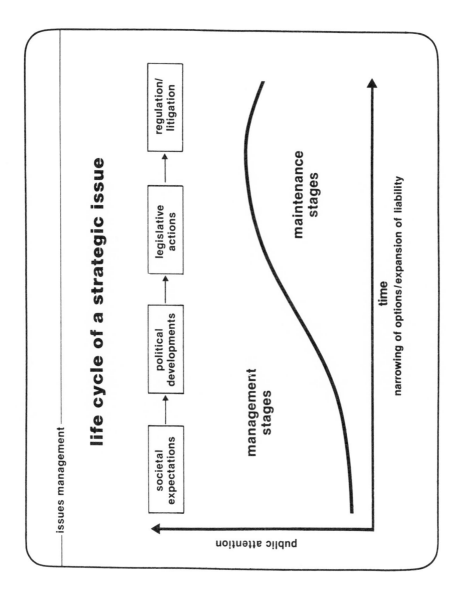

issues management

life cycle of a strategic issue

| societal expectations | → | political developments | → | legislative actions | → | regulation/ litigation |

management stages

maintenance stages

public attention

time
narrowing of options/expansion of liability

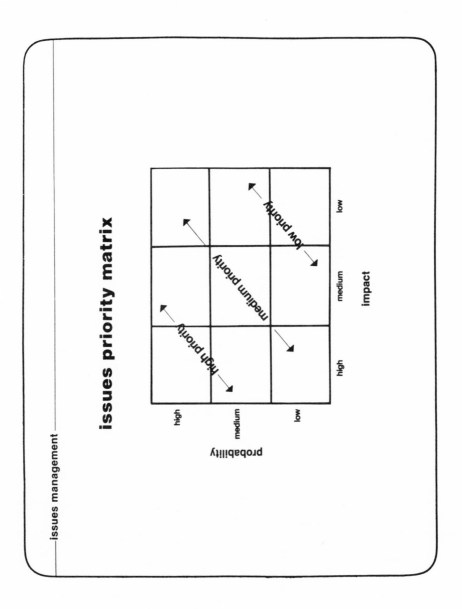

issues management

issues priority matrix

issues management process
an illustrative example*

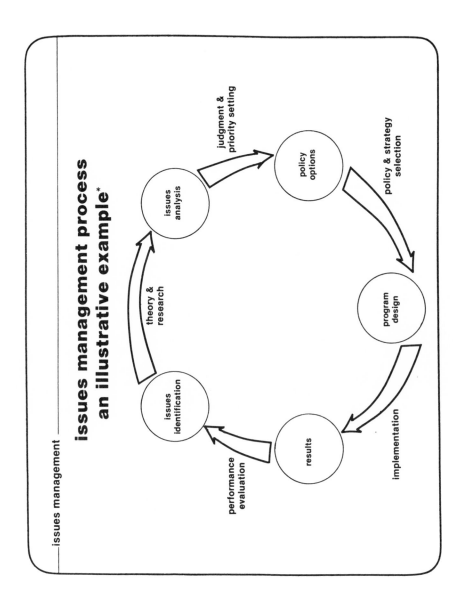

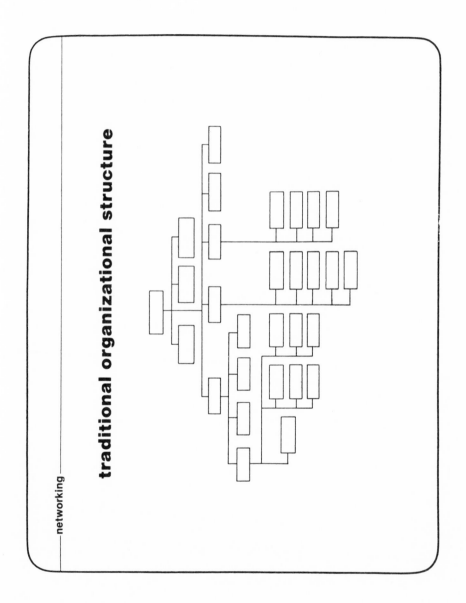

traditional organizational structure

networking

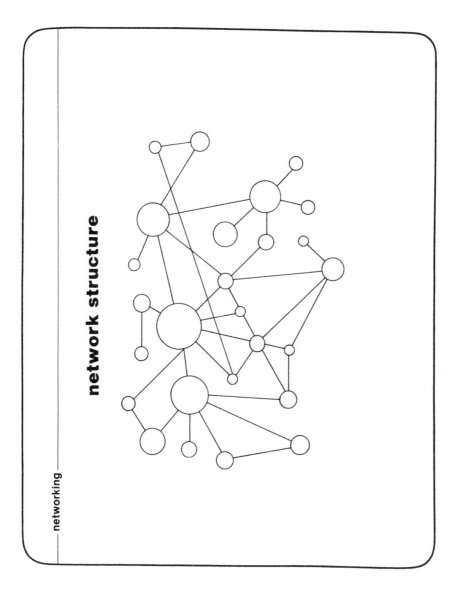

network structure

characteristics of four networks committed to foresight activities

organization	when founded	type of membership	number of members	permanent staff
the business council	1933	business executives	200	3
the council on trends and perspective (u.s. chamber of commerce)	1966	academic and business upper management	34	1
the business round table	1972	corporate ceo's	194	20
corporate associates for environmental monitoring	1976	business representatives (upper and middle management)	20	none